CW01498615

Egyptian Nag Hammadi Secrets

Retranslation, Analysis & Revision

Kevin Dermot O'Doherty

First published by Kevin Dermot O'Doherty
© 2022
All rights reserved.
ISBN: 9798842914357

All rights reserved. Except for quotations in critical articles or reviews no part of this book may be reproduced in any manner without prior written permission from the author.

The rights of Kevin Dermot O'Doherty have been asserted in accordance with the Copyright Designs and Patents Act 1988.

Book cover design and artwork by Kevin Dermot O'Doherty.

VALENTIA PRESS

DEDICATION

To the wonderful works of Sophia and all those
who have suffered by way of the archons!

CONTENTS

About the author

Kevin Dermot O'Doherty was born in Liverpool, England and has dual Irish nationality. He first became interested in the Nag Hammadi Codices (NHC) in 1997 following a BBC documentary which featured the origins of the Coptic Church in Egypt. Like many who encounter them, he found the NHC writings almost unfathomable but felt the need to reveal their strong and relevant messages for modern mankind. Invisibly guided, he embarked on a literary journey to unlock their secrets.

Kevin (formerly *West*) laid the foundation for the understanding of these texts through his forty-two years experience as a Spiritualist medium and healer. His comprehensive knowledge and ability in the fields of psychic and spiritual science have helped him bring clarity to what these texts say and teach.

He was a Spiritualist church president in Waterloo, Liverpool, UK, for many years but is no longer attached to any religion or organisation. He is also a multi-award-winning filmmaker with many hours of broadcast experience to his credit, including managing a TV studio. He was a regular on Liverpool's City Talk FM as an esoteric pundit. He has been an activist for people's rights and freedoms. He holds two black belts with the World Ju-Jitsu Federation.

CHAPTER ONE
JOURNEY INTO THE
NAG HAMMADI

There is said to be in existence a work called the Book of Great Secrets or Book of Secrets. It has oftentimes been referred to in literature throughout the ages. And of this book, the same thing is said, namely, that by reading its contents, all the answers concerning our existence will become clear. To this end, it has been searched for far and wide, and for all their efforts, none have managed to achieve its recovery. But sometimes fate lends a hand, and that is what happened along the Nile River with its unassuming discovery. The title by which it is known was given to it by the scholars who translated it.

Because this manuscript had more than one Coptic version within the Nag Hammadi Library, what follows is drawn from each of these, and hereby distilled into a single conversion. The purpose of this re-translation is to tease out, and flag up, its strong psychic and spiritual science aspects; something not understood, and so ignored, by the original translators on whose shoulders this work stands. So, to bring greater clarity, it has been necessary to expand the text without compromise to the original.

The library is a collection of 3rd and 4th-century Gnostic manuscripts discovered by a local farmer named Muhammed al-Samman in 1945 in the Nile cliffs near the Upper Egyptian town of Nag Hammadi. The originals will have dated much earlier than this. They consist of thirteen leather-bound papyrus codices buried in a sealed jar. They comprise fifty-two treatises and three works belonging to the Corpus Hermeticum, plus a partial translation of Plato's Republic. Unlike many works of this kind, they have escaped all revision and editing, and have been kept together in the Coptic Museum in Cairo.

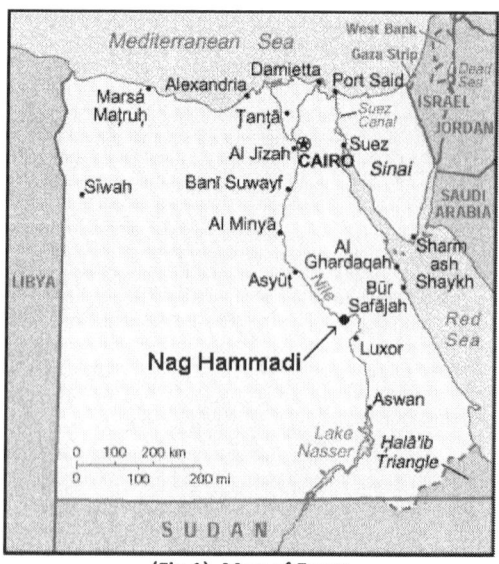

(Fig.1). Map of Egypt

For the serious student and casual enquirer alike, there is some considerable misunderstanding and misinterpretation, and dare it be said, disinformation encountered in respect of Gnosticism, i.e., what it is, and how it is defined in the NHL, if at all. And of the texts themselves, all kinds of wild assertions have been made, and as such, you may find yourself baffled by claim and counterclaim as to what these late-antiquity folios really say.

The attention of this book, however, is not to explore the diaspora of Gnosticism. Instead, you are herein offered a subjective analysis, revision, and re-translation of two of the library's key books, On the Origin of the World and Hypostasis of the Archons. They are chosen here because they are the outstanding progenitors of the collection. Like eating the fruit of the sacred trees, if you can take in what these two books offer, then the rest of the library will become all the clearer to you. To best understand them, we must approach them like a detective arriving at a crime scene cold, without any preconceptions of what we might find, and temporarily push to the side anything we might hear or be told. That way, you free yourself from the clutter of competing sources of information and instruments of persuasion whose interests lie squarely against the truth of what is inscribed.

If one is taught in accordance with one's ability to learn, then take from these texts all you can because that is the spirit in which they were written. They are not the exclusive preserve of those who originally translated them or, indeed, their overseeing institutions. They belong to the world and should be shared far and wide with those who are constituted to understand and spread their important message to humanity.

Our knowledge, and grasp, is based almost entirely upon the publishings of those who contest them. Scholars and theologians define and offer analyses within the framings of their respective institutions. Professional comprehensions and conclusions rest merely in their material component instead of what they truly disclose, namely the answer to the really big questions of who, what, why, when, where and how we are, through 'the revealing', 'the psychic' and the 'spiritual science of God'! It could be argued they are the only books in the world to do this because when it comes to questions of the eternal verities, all other disciplines and beliefs either fall silent or suddenly become inarticulate; not so the Nag Hammadi Library.

These books hold consummate knowledge of the laws that govern the vertically integrated planes of matter, ether and spirit, and how we are an integral part of creation, indeed, at the very centre of it (the status of the one true God and the heavenly aeons notwithstanding). These are the teachings of masters and exponents immersed in the understanding of auras, energies, spirits, demons, and other classes of interdimensional entities and the realms they occupy and control. And of the latter, they seek to give to us the gravest warning of 'archon' intrusion, their universal threat to us, and how these creatures emerged as a supra phantastic, super intelligent anomaly from the bile of the original womb in the predominant form of ETs. It details their part in shaping the creation of the human being as well as our social mores. They are delineated as the supreme, sabotaging influence on that which created us. Although he is only referred to in

4

these first two books, one of the principal themes of Jesus's mission, in the texts, is to remind us of their omnipresent threat and influence. Hence, he comes as the 'perfect human' to awaken the Divine Plan within.

In order to understand what is written, you must suspend much of what you think you already know, and any thoughts you may have about the order of the world and what many think of as its creator. Christian orthodox thinking has declared these books as being of 'no value' and 'ridiculous'. Jewish orthodoxy is also inclined to disregard them or cite them as containing clear evidence of Hebrew shaping, thereby rebutting the claim that Gnosticism evolved as a Christian heresy. It is the Christian voice that cries the loudest condemnation of them and, therefore, requires the greater consideration. To the well-attuned adept, codices such as the two we shall be dealing with here, are clearly much older than the papyrus on which they were written. The in-built gnosis of the enlightened enquirer will indicate that these philosophies and disciplines may well date back to the very earliest of times.

These texts wrestle with the modern reader because they were written in a different era by those who thought differently to the way we do today. Their world view was not shaped by, or immersed in, a consumerist technocracy. They rejected such worldliness. They chose, instead, to walk with, and bring forth, that which created us.

In the interests of achieving greater clarity, it has been necessary to returned to the original sources, specifically those of ancient Greek and Egyptian Coptic, to uncover their deeper truth, meaning and message for the world. From across the millennia, these writings will deliver on the promise they make to you if you are constituted to receive their message. As Jesus says in the Dialogue of the Saviour, (NHC) 'The one who sees is the one who reveals.' If you persevere you will be greatly rewarded, and your understanding of life made fuller. They will slowly reveal to you their 'great secrets'. But you are warned that this may come at a price! The interdimensional 'powers' that have conspired to keep mankind blind and locked in slavery will visit upon you prior to, during or just after your sleep state. They dread the human being becoming alive to their evil. They exist in a state of fear of being discovered any minute now. Should you come under their attack, do not fear because the exalted angel, Eleleth reveals to Norea what you should say, and do, to repel their intrusions in Chapter Three, Testament of Norea, paragraph 33.

Unfortunately, in respect of the Nag Hammadi Library overall, scholarly generosity does not extend to those with alternative forms of thinking around them. They have reserved their right to hold copyright over these works, so it has been necessary to go back afresh and retranslate them, as they were meant to be understood, within the truer, wider scope of a psychic and spiritual awareness framing – something completely ignored (as stated above) by those whose interests are to oppose them and challenge their relevance and authority in the world. But there are a significant number of professional thinkers who concord with the annotation style of this author. Furthermore, some see it as a worthy way to inspire a deeper thinking into them. They were bequeathed to us for, amongst other things, discussion, and it is hoped this book will be the start of new, broader dialogues outside their expected exclusivity.

USE OF THE HERMENEUTIC

This is a method of interpretation widely used in certain classes of texts such as biblical, wisdom literature and philosophical writings from late antiquity. This is because immediate comprehension may not always be apparent. Hermeneutics also includes the art of understanding and communicating meaning.

The term 'Archon' is the defining generic term for the authorities, the rulers, the pitiless ones, the robbers and so on. It appears throughout the NHC to describe the children and creations of the counterfeit Almighty God and is used here by the author for greater clarity, standardisation and understanding within the work.

CHAPTER TWO
'TESTAMENT OF NOREA'
(ALSO KNOWN AS 'THE FIRST ACCOUNT OF NORAIA')

For reference, Bentley Leyton's (1990) original scholarly title for the work is *The Reality/Hypostasis of the Rulers/Archons.*

According to the NHC, archons are the pre-existing, super intelligent species to the human being. In several forms they are life-sucking entities who dominate, fashion, and maintain the lower etheric and material planes. They are variously credited with creating the celestial dome of the stars, the spheres of the solar system, as well as the 'footstool' of the earth. And they made the human body and soul by replicating its form from matter, and by adhering to the template revealed to them by Pistis Sophia in her correction of their works of error. Within the NHC, they are also described as 'space conquerors', and masters of space and time. They are acknowledged overall as history's omnipresent demonic entities and ETs.

Note: '[]' Square brackets represent author comment and expansion within the texts.

Italics represent author retranslations, except where they occur in the author's own paragraphs. In those parts that are told in the first person, the voice is that of Norea/Noraia/Orea/Oraia, the biological daughter of Adam and Eve. Ultimately, authorship of the text is unknown. Norea's account is a parallax to the Eden nativity and other parts found in the *Book of Great Secrets*. It is contiguous with the *raison d'etre* of the archons, offering a deeper, wider version, and perspective on the entire garden story.

Occasionally, the use of the term archon is a replacement for where a different word occurs in the text yet means the same thing. This is to aid the reader's understanding and is in keeping with the original translation.

> 1. *Here is the truth of the archons, told here with words that are inspired by the* power *of the father of truth.* The great apostle [in] referring to the "*archons* of the *blindness*" - *said to* us that "our *fight* is not *with* flesh and blood; *but with*, the a*rchons* of the universe and the *spirits of wickedness."

*Archons live in 'error' and so do certain spirits. Jesus discusses these 'spirits of error' in the Judas codex, and they are also referenced in the *Book of Great Secrets.*

The *great apostle* is Paul, though more recently it has been suggested the Epistle to the Ephesians was not written in AD 62, but rather in AD 80-100 by a different author adopting his style. This is a wonderful example of how the NHC can forensically clear up this contentious scholarly debate by virtue of this one line making it clear that authorship of Ephesians belongs to Paul – another nail in the coffin of the NHC being 'worthless' and 'ridiculous.' Remember, these texts have escaped all revision, are predominantly written on both sides of the folios and are without redaction, correction, or annotation. For the record, Paul was not a true apostle. He never even met Jesus.

> I have sent this (to you) because you *ask* about the *truth* of the *archons*.

In the last part of this codex, Norea records in great detail her battle with the archons and what it is that humans can do to successfully repel them. The version in the book of the New Testament, Ephesians 6: 12, states similarly, *'For we wrestle not against flesh and blood, but against* **principalities***, against* **powers***, against the* **rulers** *of the darkness of this world, against spiritual wickedness in high places'* [in this context meaning on the lower-order etheric plane].

In the NHC, these are all terms used to describe archons. And *spiritual wickedness* seems to echo what Jesus tells Judas (as mentioned above) that some spirits are majorly led astray. The oft used term, *darkness* has several meanings including that of the void of chaos from which matter eventually emerged through the power of Pistis.

The scholarly interpretive distortions in Ephesians are hereby offered an alternative explanation that is more in keeping with Norea's experience. Archon means prince or ruler, hence *principality,* a territory ruled by a prince or princess. It is also the position, sovereignty, authority, or jurisdiction of a prince or princess. Its significance in this quote can be found in how the word draws from the same root stem for monarch (*mono-archon*) which was used as a reference to foreign [or alien] princes who had rule over such regions. So, our fight is not with societal institutions, rather the inter-dimensional, off-world powers. This bold statement shall become more apparent as we progress through the narrative.

> 2. *The chief of the archons is without sight or the blessing of reason. Because of his dominance, his ignorance and his self-importance, he spoke through his power and said, "I am the one and only God; there is none other." But overlooking him from on high, the Spirit was greatly offended by this and voiced, "You are wrong, Samael", meaning* god of the blind!

> 3. *Samael's thinking* [had] *become blind.* And having *boasted* his *dominance,* that is *to say,* the *outrage* he had *uttered* - he *declared* it [throughout the void and the realm of shadow/darkness].

The terms shadow and darkness are not necessarily pejoratives any more than is the term, matter.

SYSTEM OF VERTICALLY INTEGRATED PLANES PECULIAR TO THE TRIPARTITE HUMAN BEING

The lower nightmare level of the astral plane is situated beneath the material plane of the earth, though perhaps not literally. It is not to be taken as hell because that is defined as a different place and ruled over by Lucifer, or 'Adam of the Luminaries'. The substance of shadow is stable and of a higher order to that of matter which is subject to decay, and hence, unstable, or 'corruptible'. And so it is that the earth plane sits beneath the astral plane which sits beneath the planes of the spirit. That is the order of things peculiar to the tripartite human being.

The NHC authors, and Natural Spiritualists, regard the earth plane as a lower aspect of the spirit world and creation of the Godhead. Humans can navigate between the first three, i.e., the one above and the one below. But the fourth plane is accessed only upon the death of the physical body, and only then if that life has been characterised by good works on the part of genuine motive. But the archons are limited by their nature and the substances of which they are made, merely to the first two, ether and matter. They cannot enter the higher aspect of the astral plane or the spirit world proper because, as quoted later in this text, 'they lacked a spiritual element within them' - *given that* beings *who* merely *have* a soul *are unable to seize* [comprehend or understand] those that *have* a spirit - for *from below they were...'*

Only the human spirit can access beyond the astral into the realms of the purer spirit or spirit world because it is from here that Sophia and Jesus tell us we have originated. But there is also a warning for the human being. In order for your spirit to achieve ascension back into the realm of the spirit, you are required to have led a life consistent with the values of one possessing a spiritual nature, and or innocence.

Archons exercise most control over the lower nightmare half of the astral where the soul-trapped spirits of humans who have been soiled by their influence can find themselves after the death of their physical body. To be more specific, it only applies to those who have *knowingly* 'erred' or created sin, and in so doing have made victims of the innocent by way of loss, harm or damage through their actions and deeds. True 'discerners of spirits', and those similarly constituted, such as spiritual healers, may go through the veil and enter this lower half for the purposes of administering 'soul rescue' and spiritual healing. These people are instruments who possess a particular developed quality of the spirit that enables them to reach those trapped in such circumstance and who, notwithstanding the law of spirit, can still be considered to have appropriate redeeming qualities, thereby fulfilling the principle of psychic science that eternal progress is open to every human soul. However, it is also important at this stage in the work to make the distinction that the power the archons exercise over the soul is derived from conscious (and possibly unconscious) consent on the part of the individual, meaning one need not have gnosis of them to do their works any more than one need have gnosis of the Entire Creator to do good works.

In the Judas codex we are told by Jesus that if you do the work of the archons (whether you know them or not) you will find yourself delivered to them, that is 'the authorities', upon the death of your physical body.

Archon control is drawn from fear and error, meaning wrong-doing, and derives its power from error and wrongdoing on the part of the freewill that springs eternal from the soul-endowed human spirit.

When it comes to the level of the earth plane, their dominance is realised as fashioners and maintainers and human archenemies. Their role in the lower astral, or nightmare plane, is defined in the *Book of Great Secrets* under the Egyptian goddess, *Justice Maat*. Those who fail to balance her scales are collected by the archons and left to comply with three core options under the natural order. Firstly, they may find themselves reincarnated after an appropriate span of earth time. Alternatively, they may become earthbound, haunting the material plane as so-called 'lost' spirits or ghosts. Or they can find themselves dwelling under the terror of the archons in the lower nightmare aspect of the etheric plane. Wherever they finish up, it is through and by their own hand, aided and abetted by archon influence, such being a source of nourishment to the latter. (See Glossary – Sin).

His mother [is Sophia] *who was* Pistis [the personification and manifestation of the Creator's power, control, fluidity, and phenomena right] *from* the *start*. And she [through and by him] *created all* of his *children* (archons) in *accordance* with *this* power [and] *in accordance with* the *model* of the *worlds* that are *higher*, [meaning as a lower order copy of the pure spirit realm fashioned out of the stellar medium, and forces of the celestial, to resemble that which was above].

SOPHIA'S FREETHINKING, ENTREPRENUERIAL NATURE

But we are given another parallax perspective in this codex; one that suggests Sophia looked out from her pleroma across her creation in much the same way we ourselves might look out from our dwelling to the perimeter of our land, thinking, 'dreaming' or imagining how we might make or fashion something with it, out of it, for it. Extending the metaphor further, a talented sculptor might take almost any material of the earth and fashion and form from it something resembling their version of a reality in which they themselves are immersed. Children, by way of innocence, are artisans of imagination, by way of play, when it comes to creating and modelling worlds, moulding characters, and giving to them all manner of situations and conditions peculiar to their experience of things. In short, we breathe life into that which we create and give to that same thing our own characteristics. One of the lessons of the texts we would do well to remember is that our thoughts and dreams *can* become our realities - so make them pure!

And so, on a cosmic scale, the NHC is telling us she would make and fashion a world just like her ennead (9th heaven) to resemble the higher creation, or spirit world, like a 'reflection' but made instead from the foundations of matter and ether. And into this fashioned world she would put not only a spiritual component to live and operate throughout, but also something of herself; her unique, freethinking, enterprising spirit - something of which the demiurge and his created retinue were deficient. Hence, from the unseen spirit world the *seen* world was *fashioned*.

SOPHIA BEGINS HER CLEANSING OF THE SHADOW AND MATERIAL PLANES

4. As *Sophia fixed her gaze* [meaning her power and influence] *below* into the *expanse*, her *reality became visible* in the [embryonic] waters; and the archons of the darkness *grew infatuated with* her. But they could not seize [*devise nor contrive*] that image, which had *become visible* to them in the *cosmic fluid, for the reason* of their *inferiority* [meaning 'they lacked a spiritual element within them'] - *given that* beings *who* merely *have* a soul *are unable to seize* [comprehend or understand] those that *have* a spirit - for *from below they were, and from above she was. For* this reason, *Sophia fixed her gaze* [meaning her powerful vision, influence, and will, was directed] *below* into the *expanse* [to become her reality and modelled creation]: so that [*through and*] by *her* Father's *order*, she *could take* the entirety [of this area of chaos] into *one* with the light.

And so, begins the first part of the destruction of the archons, thereby addressing a problem she would appear to have made for herself; some might say unintentionally. It is important that we now return to her original thought in generating a womb in which to grow the spirit foetuses of all manner of gods and deities. It would seem that the unanticipated fluid residue of that womb, namely shadow and matter, and the emergence of a demiurge, was not part of her original plan. And if that is so, then neither could the later creation of the human being!

Sophia's next step was to correct the problem by making the demiurge 'a princely ruler' over these planes. She then returned to her home in the 9th heaven where she dwells with her counterpart and male equivalent, the aeon Christos. But this apparent pre-human remedy fails to ameliorate the perceived problem. The demiurge and his negative angel retinue soon grow to become like an infection or malignancy throughout it.

We are told that the hierarchy above are far from pleased when the demiurge declares to his angels that he is the one and only creator and responsible for all the perceived phenomena. To fulfil her desire to *'bring the entirety of her creation into one with the light'*, these rogue entities will have to be removed or rendered impotent through their fatal flaw, i.e., their obsession with spirit per se. And so, she reveals the template for the human being, a species similar to them insomuch as being anthropoid, and constituted to be like a sweet, irresistible poison or slave species introduced into their hive so as to destroy them from within.

It will be born of her spirit to incarnate in a shadow and matter form so as to occupy the same planes as those they will 'ruin'. The human being will have to be physical and possess a soul endowed tree system, but one that will significantly differ from the archons in that it will be the perfect and exclusive vehicle for her light. But for this to happen she must, as it were, deceive the demiurge into creating the desired model. And for this plan (See Glossary, Divine Mission Plan) to work, its material configuration must, at the same time, differ significantly from that of the archons in order that these elemental creatures of shadow and matter will *not* be able to live alongside the human being in a physical form. For this physical aspect to happen, the toxic, lightless surface of the demiurge's 'footstool', *Earth,* and the seven spheres of the hebdomad, will have to be transformed. As described in the *Book of Great Secrets,* Sabaoth (also known as *Lucifer* and Adam of the Luminaries), who was one of the Seven Great Archons (spheres), became a bright, life-giving sun with the aid of his wife, Eve (Zoe, whose name means *life*).

So, it came to be that the earth would be transformed into a bio realm that is noxious to archons. The Anthropos shall be made of a different biological and physiological arrangement to them and shall be in a form explicit to hosting (we) her 'little innocent spirits'. But she also knows that in this pre-human world, the archons of shadow and matter will become a barrier to them returning to her after the death of their physical bodies. She knows the life of the human being will be characterised by alien and demonic interference from the start. Not all will make it back to the spirit realm safely for the sake of human freewill and choice. Some will fall prey to the influence of the beings of the darkness. That is why Sophia is the embodiment of forgiveness and her name means love. She knows only too well what challenges, trials and dilemmas will face us on earth. So, when the text says,

> 5. When it says the archons *devised* a *plan*
> and *held*, "*We shall model, [shape and form]*
> a man made [*in her image*] from the
> *material of the* earth" - it is really saying
> they merely thought they did for the sake of

Sophia's deception, magisterial control, and manipulation of them.

Some have asked, why not simply let the archons flourish in their dimensions of shadow and matter? What harm could they possibly do? For, as we understand it, humans do not figure in Sophia's creation at this point until our template is revealed during the transformation of the solar system. This makes sense of what Jesus says in the *Sophia Wisdom of Jesus Christ,* that the human being (part of you) is purely a thing of the earth. What seems beyond dispute is that she wants the archons destroyed, and we will be her desired instrument of destruction. And if she accepts ultimate responsibility for the entirety of her creation then, as one would expect, she will masterfully create something to tear it down for no less a reason than it is the antithesis of all she embodies and all that is Divine. She will therefore, '*take* the entirety [of this area of chaos] into *one* with the light,' (Paragraph 4).

We like to know not only from where we have come but also why we are here; something for which the NHC offers a plausible explanation. No other works in the world enlighten you about this, and if they do then certainly not to this extent or with such accomplished authority. That is why the NHC is unique. That is why its message needs to be offered far and wide. That is why they were buried by the knowledgeable ones and kept hidden by fate for so long, just waiting to be rediscovered and re-revealed to the world of dying humankind.

THE ARCHONS ARE TRICKED INTO CREATING THE

HUMAN BEING (ANTHROPOS) FROM SOPHIA'S TEMPLATE

Hence, they *fabricated* their *mortal* [*creation*] as one *completely* of the world *and using the material of* the earth and *shaped* a *human comparable* to them in *their physical structure,* and *comparable* also to the *figure* of Sophia [meaning her sacred trees] *which* [pattern] had *become visible* to them *within* the waters. They *held,* "[And] *We shall imprison* it by *drawing* [her spirit] to the *manly figure* we have *sculptured.*"

Here we see their arrogance displayed; born of catastrophic blindness as to the nature of Sophia, their mother, their generator, and that which is of her will. Ignorant of their part in her mission plan, they think they can imprison and capture her Spirit and hence the spirits she creates. So how is it that this supra intelligent species fails to know or understand the nature of what has been revealed to them on the very planes over which they are 'masters' and 'rulers'? An explanation is offered further back in the text where it states, '...*given that* beings *who* merely *have* a soul *are unable to seize* those that *have* a spirit - for *from below they are...*' But also consider this. The world is awash with intelligent people who are completely ignorant and blind, not only to their true Creator but also to the spirit that lives within them. Suffice it to say, the world is replete with accomplished atheists and agnostics.

They *held,* "Come, *we shall seize* it *with the use* of the *figure which* we have *made,* so that it *might perceive* its *masculine equal* [...in that form],"

They have, in effect, produced a kind of dormant or non-functioning anthropoid. We can only speculate as to its true appearance. But it is a real, living thing of the earth, and like our living world, it must have had something of Sophia's beauty, resemblances, and similarities.

"...and we *might take hold of* it with the *figure* that we have *sculptured*" - not *knowing* the *efficacious control* of God, because of their [inferiority and] *inability*. And *by* *breathing into his face [thereby giving him physical life], the *manly figure became possessed of* a soul..."

*The Greek word for soul is derived from a verb, *to cool, to blow*, and hence refers to the vital breath, the animating principal in humans and other animals.

THE SOUL (OR SHADOW)
The psychic is of the soul - the spirit is of the Spirit.

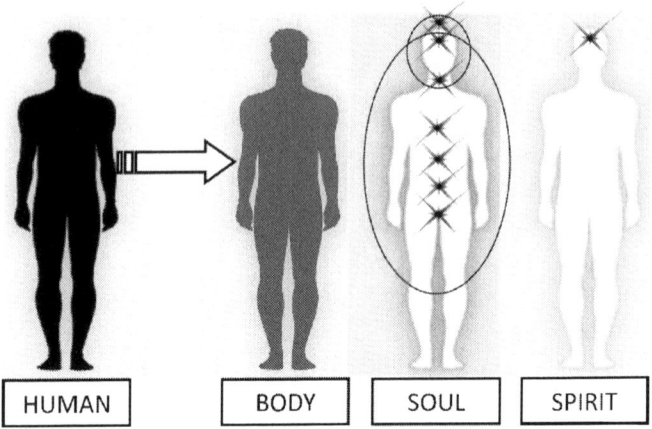

| HUMAN | BODY | SOUL | SPIRIT |

(Fig. 2) Soul illustration.

Matter is unstable and subject to decay, hence *corruptible*. However, the energy and substance of which the soul is made is etheric; made of what the Essenes call 'the subtlest ether'. It is a supra complex energy form and contains within it the blueprint for the physical body. The substance of the soul *can* be immortal, but not beyond alteration. It is a vehicle or vessel for the human spirit. And, like the archons who have created him, this example of a hermaphrodite Anthropos (soon to be named Adam), is lacking the faculty of a consciousness, intellect, or mind.

As described by Natural Spiritualism, the soul is merely a thing of the lower, middle and higher planes and not a thing of the plane of spirit. Reverend G. Maurice Elliott wrote in his book, *'When Prophets Spoke, Spiritualism in the Old Testament'*, that Adam is a plural Hebrew word that means 'mankind'. So, in the generation of the *Adam creature,* we have an intelligence that is like a computer, meaning enabled with power and a hard drive, but deficient of the software to run it. Therefore,

> "... [and *stayed*] *lying on* the *earth a lot of* days. They *failed in their attempts to* make him *awaken by virtue* of their [weakness and] *inability*. Like *a blizzard* they *continued blowing* [meaning soul generation, in order] to [seize and take possession of, and replicate] that image, which *materialised for* them *within* the *cosmic flow*. And they *failed to* [perceive or understand as fact or truth] ...the identity [nature and origin] of its power.

Many mythologists, including alternative ones, have put forward the view that Sophia has operated without permission, independent of the Creator of the Entirety. However, as we can see in the following passage, this is not so.

> 6. *Every part of this occurred* by the *determination* of the *Creator* of the *Entirety*.

In the NHC, Sophia's story can be read in two ways; *all is known,* and *all is not known*. When one considers the consistent theme of Sophia's *forethought,* the outcomes of all she sets in motion must already be recognised and calculated. This line could be seen as a verification amid the chaos of the unfolding story, that at least the Eternal, Self-Generated Creator (big God) exercises an efficient and effective control over all these developments.

Philosophically, in relation to the systemising of the world, a mountaintop séance in the *Sophia Wisdom of Jesus Christ* codex records Philip asking the post-corporeal re-materialised Jesus: "[What is] *the underlying reality of the universe and the plan, Master."* Jesus replies, *"Those blessed with the gifts of wisdom and insight have hypothesised on the organising of the world and its progress. But their speculations have fallen short of the truth. Where philosophers are concerned, the organisation of the world is focussed in three ways with none amongst them being of the same mind. For concerning the world, a number say that it organises itself. Others, it is organised by providence. Others, it is organised by fate or destiny, none of which are true, **for these are all concepts that come from man.**"*

What is not recognised by scholars of the NHC is that the *Book of Great Secrets* and *Testament of Norea,* are themselves a description of the Divine Mission Plan and revelation of *great secrets!*

> *Later*, the *spirit caught sight* of the *soul-given* man upon the *surface of the earth.* And *she drew* forth *as of* the Adamantine Land (the material earth); [she] *moved* it *down* and [it] came to *reside inside* him, and that man *developed* into a soul *that had life* [meaning a connection with the aeon spirit]. It [the daughter of Pistis Sophia, Zoe] *gave him the* name Adam, *given that* he was *discovered in motion on* the *surface of the earth.*

Returning to the *Sophia Wisdom of Jesus Christ*, there is a passage in which he makes an interesting philosophical point. He is quoted defining the Creator of the Entirety as being without a **name**, *'For that which has a name has been created by another.'* The only one not created by another is the Entire Creator, and therefore the Creator is without a name. So here we see the aeon spirit, by way of Sophia's daughter, Zoe (the 1st Eve and meaning 'life'), claiming a type of ownership and responsibility in respect of the flawed 'Adam' product. This is further realised in the following part.

A *desire and wish emerged* from incorruptibility [the aeon realm] for the *succour* [meaning, assistance, comfort, aid and sustenance] of Adam; and the *archons drew* together *every* animal of the earth and *every fowl* of heaven and *took* them to Adam [so as] to *learn* what **name** Adam would give *to* each *one* of them, *fowls* and *animals*.

*See Glossary – Eros.

7. *Into the *garden they placed Adam so that he might plant* it and *keep vigil* over it.

*Garden, gar-den, meaning Gaia Eden. (French) Jardin, jar (gar.), meaning earthen vessel of water, meaning the earth, meaning the 'garden' is the *earth, vessel of water, and Eden* - the earth, essentially, being of the waters.

Then comes the imperative deception played by the archons on the naive creature, Adam.

> The *archons made* a *demand upon* him, saying, "*You may eat from any tree in the garden except* from the tree of *knowing* [the difference between] good and evil [right and wrong]. Do not *consume* [or be filled by], nor *have contact with* it; for the day you *ingest of* its [fruit], *shall you* die.*"

In the newly created brain intelligence of Adam, they implanted a psychological fear stratagem that he shall die should he go against their command. And, as with a naive child, the archons found it easy to place a fear upon him, one he dares not transgress. They are his only source of information and influence. As examples of humanity, we pride ourselves on *knowing* the distinctions between good and evil - right and wrong. They seek to exercise an exclusive power over him as a forerunner to the access and control they have over the human today.

> 8. [Deeper author retranslation of incoherent text]: They do not understand [the full import] *of their order* to him [meaning, they are falling ever deeper into Sophia's trap]. Rather, [they think it is] *by the will of the demiurge* [that] they [said] this *to Adam so as to trap or trick, or strongly influence him into eating from the tree* [so he might fall from his state of grace, thereby providing

them with a pretext for his removal because of his newfound potential for enlightenment]. *And they accomplished this in such a way as to make him think they had authority over him, and at the same time causing him to now view the world fearfully instead of innocently.*

THE CREATION OF THE MALE & FEMALE

9. [So] the *Archons contrived with* one *another*, and *held*, "Come, *we shall* cause a *profound* sleep to *descend* upon Adam." And *his eyes closed.* - Now the *profound* sleep *which* they "caused to *descend over* him, and he slept" is [the Curse of] Ignorance.

An androgynous being contains an equal balance of both male and female.

(Fig. 3) Yaldabaoth splits the androgyne to progress his seed through the womanly half.

> They *unlocked* his *sphere* [meaning they split into two halves, that part of the androgynous Adam] *resembling* a living woman. And they *increased* his *half* with some flesh [a penis] in place of her [half, meaning, privy part or womb], and Adam *became blessed merely* with soul.

This passage concerning the unlocking of the male/female sphere of Adam, thereby creating the two genders, has echoes of a pioneering surgical procedure conducted by the insane Dr. Money on a twin baby called David Reimer in 1967. A botched circumcision meant he had been left without a penis. At twenty-two months he was 'gender reassigned' through the removal

28

of his testicles and given the name Brenda. Although the surgical creation of a vagina was recommended, this was not carried out, but he *was* put on a course of hormone treatment and brought up in *ignorance* as a woman. This *experiment,* needless to say, was a colossal failure. He never made the transition into a female. And through the photo pornographic exploitation, medical and psychological intermeddling of the doctor, he and his twin eventually took their own lives. Sadly, because of his fabrications, countless *full* gender reassignments were subsequently performed as a direct result. Based on this analysis, the NHC nativity of Adam was genetic, whereas Dr. Money's procedure was purely surgical. Through no fault of his own, and before he could consent or comprehend, David Reimer's body was modified counter to the orientation of the two other component parts that made up his tripartite, i.e., his soul and his spirit which were male. Dr. Money could be said to be the perfect human personification of an archon instrument.

EVE, THE MOTHER OF THE MORTAL

10. And the spirit-*gifted female form drew close* and *said*, "*Awaken*, Adam, *and begin your life.*" And when he *perceived* her, he *held*, "*You have gifted* me *mortal existence*; you *shall* be *known as the* 'mother of the *mortal*'. - *Because* she is my mother. [He added], She [this female form, this energy of the spirit] is the physician *of nature*, and [of] the [human] woman [womb man, or man with a womb], and she *is the one* who has *gifted* [me] *nativity*."

11. *Afterwards,* the archons *approached* their Adam. *They discerned* his female *equivalent, sharing and talking* with him, *and* they *grew troubled* with *immense anxiety*; [but at the same time] they *also grew infatuated with* her. They *held* to *each other*, "Come, *we shall implant* our seed in her," and they *chased* her [trying to capture her mystery].

The term *chased* is used a number of times and can be taken to signify their attempts to know, understand and decode.

ARCHON FAILURE TO UNDERSTAND HOW THE SPIRIT ANIMATES THE BODY

Many have said this part of the narrative is an example of Sophia's mastery of the genome, the human DNA, i.e., that she has placed something in our genetic code that the archons cannot possibly decipher. And this is why a particular aspect of them, for example the androgynous ETs, continue to conduct the same experiment on us time and time again without apparent progress. In *Confrontations*, p.13, the renowned Dr. Jaques Valles puts forward the idea that the so-called 'medical examination' suffered by abductees includes 'sadistic sexual manipulation'. He likens it to the demons encountered in the Euro-Gaelic/English folk tales of the medieval era and points out that for all their super intelligence, sophistication, 'technical framework' and 'marvels', surely, they could have just as easily achieve their 'alleged objectives' quicker and with less 'risk'.

It is also worth pointing out that he did not see UFOs as interstellar, rather local. They usually had a single or small number of occupants and were ill-equipped to travel in the depths of outer space. For that they would require a much larger mothership. But if the NHC accounts are to be understood in this respect, it is clear the archons dwell within the earth and the solar system.

Students of these texts will note that the key region of interest for ETs is the kundalini root chakra access point of the human physical and soul body, which also houses our reproductive faculty. But this oft accepted special code theory behind the alien abduction phenomena is fatally flawed because the NHC is explicit in telling us the archons replicated and enacted the code! Archon 'deficiency' is found only in respect of how the spirit component of the 'tripartite' human is able to animate the body and soul.

What is more, the NHC is absolutely clear that the archons are the ones set up to make and manufacture organic and soul life. In the *Apocryphon of John* it is stated that they generated *'seven powers for themselves'*, each linked to a *'limb'* of the human body or chakra of the soul. These *'powers'*, in turn, generated *'for themselves six angels for each one'* totalling *'(360 or) 365 angels'* [meaning demons, meaning energies and forces], *'until'* the human physical *'body was completed by them'*.

360 represents all the ways we can move and see, i.e., up, down, left, right, sideways, backwards, and straight ahead. 365 represents every day of the year, meaning they are masters of space and time and control every human soul.

The *Gospel of Mary Magdalene* is essentially a post crucifixion materialisation séance in which the etheric form of Jesus appears to the disciples through the physical trance of Mary; she being the supremely gifted spirit medium of the disciples. At the end of the séance, she 'arises', meaning she comes out of her trance, or altered state. Upon request, she then recounts a lesson taught to her by Jesus with regard to the nature, origin and character of the soul. He held it as a *'space conqueror'* and something that can be used to control the human spirit by reason of its strong archon influence, ruled over through and by the hand of the demiurge. He originally sabotaged it to *become a prison for the light* [meaning human spirit]. The archons are fully aware that a created human body and soul will attract a spirit into it. By reason of this, a significant part of their overall flawed plan is revealed. They are, in effect, creating the vessels to house the 'little innocent spirits' that (they realise) will ultimately destroy them.

In the Judas codex, a worried Judas asks Jesus, "Master, *is it possible for* my root [referring to the root chakra entry point of his tree], *to be* under the control of the *archons*?" Hence, when it comes to discovering how the incarnated spirit operates and inhabits the systems of the tripartite human, scholars, and alternative mythologists alike, are disadvantaged; left to blindly display their lack of understanding in relation to the laws and principles of psychic and spiritual science and, instead, stick to liturgy and speculation within the framings of their respective disciplines.

And she [being from above] *laughed at them [meaning they were unable to break her and have ownership of her] for *their lack of sense, comprehension and judgement* [in thinking they could lay hold of and understand her spirit].

*A professor in a laboratory may come to feel that nature is laughing and mocking his lack of understanding, comprehension, or poverty of knowledge concerning the problem in front of him - mocking him for his lack of equivalence - awakening and wounding the pride of his ego.

> *And she mocked* their *loss of sight;* and *under* their *control* she *turned into* a [sacred] *tree [of life]* ...

*Which was the next step of her plan. She *mocks* them because they are happy and confident of their control over the substances of ether and matter. Through her manipulation, blindly they begin to exploit her Wisdom to make something that will ultimately bring about their predestined destruction; namely, the teachable, responsive, freethinking, spirit-endowed human being. This wonderful connivance finds them constructing the tree matrix of the Anthropos which will systemise and animate the flesh and become a vehicle for the many *little innocent spirits* she will send.

> ...and left *facing* them her *dark and indistinct* [difficult to understand] reflection [that was] *similar to* herself; and they *corrupted* it *hideously.*

This is the enormous, loveless defiling of the sacred image of Sophia's creation pattern for the Anthropos, and the archons' pursuit of it could be considered comparable to the way 'robbers' might steal and replicate a template for the purposes of counterfeiting and generating their own wealth at the expense of the authentic original.

> And they *corrupted* the stamp of her *influence*, so that by the *figure* they had *replicated*, *jointly* with their [own] *likeness*, they [in ignorance] *condemned* themselves.

DO ARCHONS LEARN?

As the demons and ETs of legend, hive-like in their mindset, it would appear they have no more knowledge today than they did before the genesis of the earth. Perhaps they are no more teachable or responsive than the insects and collective creatures with which their hierarchy shares a model. Hence, these super elemental, super intelligent creatures of sophistication appear destined to repeat their experiments over and over again at the expense of naked humanity. They appear incapable of higher spiritual human emotions such as love and understanding but know only too well the power of fear and intimidation. Thus, they have no empathy or love but are obsessive masters at eliciting the same from their victims through artificial means in much the same way psycho drugs can mimic a plethora of human emotions. Consequently, they can make their victims feel love, fear, eroticism, or ecstasy - indeed anything so as to take from them that which they need.

It is by these means they display their immense predatory and parasitic qualities. In the *Book of Enoch* and in the *Book of Great Secrets*, the Watchers (archons who breakaway from the demiurge) are credited with giving to humans the skills necessary to make all manner of 'potions' and 'libations' to curse the Anthropos with dependencies, addictions, and negative drives, thereby distracting them from the Divine.

THE 'INSTRUCTING' SERPENT SNAKE

And before we go any further, let us define the snake in terms of this codex. An 'instructor' empowers and informs through a transition from ignorance to enlightenment, the appropriately constituted body or human.

(Fig. 4) System of the soul.

As a houn, Kundalini means snake. As an adjective it means annular or coiled. The Kundalini is characterised by the serpent or snake, but as those well versed in the disciplines of psychic and spiritual science know, it is much more than that. Whether as a coil, single or double helix, it symbolises the transceiving of natural and spiritual energy. In Sanskrit it signifies the divine feminine corporeal spiritual power that dwells within the human and can be awakened in order to purify and create a state of divine union between the one and the One. The Upanishads describe it as a coiled, divine, feminine snake goddess lying, as it were, unconscious like an intuitive libido energy in the loin chakra. Once awakened it rises through the seven organs of the etheric astral body to reside within the crown chakra of the head. Under the right conditions it is possible for psychics and sensitives to visibly discern this phenomenon through their own brow chakra, or psychic third eye, as a luminous radiance around the head of an enlightened one. Early religious depictions of Jesus, the saints, prophets, and martyrs in art were a clear reference to this nimbus gloriosity.

Next, we need to consider Adam and Eve in the codex. Firstly, the Old Testament and generic cross-faith orthodox view lacks the detail and convolution of the NHC versions of their story. Simple mainstream research of pertinent material shows two things. Firstly, that neither scholar, Christian nor Abrahamic can agree amongst themselves as to which version in Genesis is the definitive. And secondly, the NHC account is completely ignored despite its impressive concordance across all the books in which it occurs and in how it plugs the gaping holes in the accepted pedestrian version.

ADAM AND EVE OF THE OLD TESTAMENT

To better understand the account in the NHC, a moment should be spend being reacquainted with the accepted version. In this respect, orthodoxy posits that it was God who created the circumstances that occurred in the Garden of Eden to test Adam. Sometimes overlooked is the fact there were two trees from which he was forbidden to eat, those of *knowledge* and *life*. If orthodox thinking is correct in maintaining that God's motive was to teach Adam a lesson, then it goes without saying He would have already known the outcome. And for that to be true, Adam must then be considered a freethinking man in his own right at the time of its occurrence. They say he failed to resist temptation thereby signifying *he* did not trust God.

Others say that after eating the fruit, Adam and Eve *understood* evil by reason of their disobedience, meaning that before the fact was good, and after the fact was guilt and shame, causing them to hide from God's view; unable to face Him. Therefore, disobeying God is evil. But if we are to accept the orthodox version, then what we are dealing with might reasonably be considered a minor misdemeanour followed by a wholly disproportionate punishment enacted by a punitive God. On this latter point, scholars, and rabbis, with glibness, have argued that if the first sin was as serious as say, murder, then the story of humanity would have been short lived! Hence God's choice of the lesser crime of defiance. In their version, Adam and Eve's perceived sin was to put each other above God. The latter by means of tempting fruit; the other by means of wife over God.

The Snake

Now we are familiar with the orthodox narrative, let us move on to the snake. The *serpent* is a high order, intelligent, divine power and energy form which is like electricity to the spiritual counterpart of the physical. And like electricity, it follows the natural laws of connection, transmission and flow through a correctly constituted channel or vessel. What cannot be denied is that it was venerated by all ancient cultures; not as a demon but as a god energy (not entity) of Divine creation power. For instance, the builders of the pyramid cities of South and Central America created their structures with the image of the plumed serpent deeply incorporated into their sacred geometry, and often depicted flying to and from the galactic cloud. Native North Americans venerated the snake too. But to orthodox religion it is a symbol of fear and dread; something to be despised instead of acknowledged as the form, shape, and pattern of the single most powerful force in the nature of the universe, the coil and the double helix.

Carnal

Compared to the orthodox canon, the NHC shows a clear, unequivocal contrary bias towards women. By scholars choosing the adjective *carnal* in the next passage to describe the female (and to a lesser extent the male) subject, it allows consideration to be given to any number of pejoratives. In the kindest sense it could be argued that it simply means *flesh woman*. So why have translators chosen this word? Is it another example of Christo Judeo male bias haemorrhaging onto the page?

12. The female spiritual principle [Zoe, daughter of Sophia] came in the [form of the] snake, [with her son] the instructor [Satan]; and [together they] taught them. [After which Satan] *asked*, "What did he say?" [They did not reply, so he then asked,] "Was it, *you can eat the fruits from any tree in the garden except from the two trees of recognising good and evil?'*

13. The *woman of flesh held,* "*Neither eat it nor touch it; because* the day you *do, by loss* [of innocence] you shall die," *is what he said.*

14. And the *reptile*, the *teacher*, [second Adam (Satan) who was created by Lucifer and Zoe to lead the humans away from the demiurge for the sake of Sophia's Mission Plan] *reassured her saying*, "*By loss* you *will* not die; *because* it was *from* [envy] that he *told* you *these things. Instead*, your *vision will* [become] *clear* [and enlightened] and you *will* come to *know, as do the gods, the difference between that which is* evil and *that which is* good." *Then* the *woman's* instructing *code* was *carried* away from the snake, *leaving* it behind, *purely* a thing of the *earth*.

15. And *Eve*, the *flesh* woman took from the [sacred] tree [of life and knowing]; and she [being the dominant] *administered* to her husband *and* herself; and these [human] beings *who* [at this stage] *had* only a soul, ate [meaning they were filled by instruction,

enlightenment, and awakening]. And their [material] imperfection became *clear* in their *absence* of knowledge; and they *realised their nakedness* [lacking] of the spiritual element and *seized* fig leaves [from the sacred tree] and *fastened* them *over* their loins.

The red coloured base chakra, where resides the oft dormant coil of the kundalini, is situated in religion's taboo area, the loin. It rises through the centre of the spirit aura, the one which extends furthest from the physical body and its vibratory energy can be felt upon the spinal column.

UNDERSTANDING THE LANGUAGE CODE OF THE EDEN STORY

To better understand what is happening in the garden, or Earth Eden, we need to see the *tree*, its *leaves*, its *fruit,* and the act of *eating* as metaphors rather than literal translations. So let us recap.

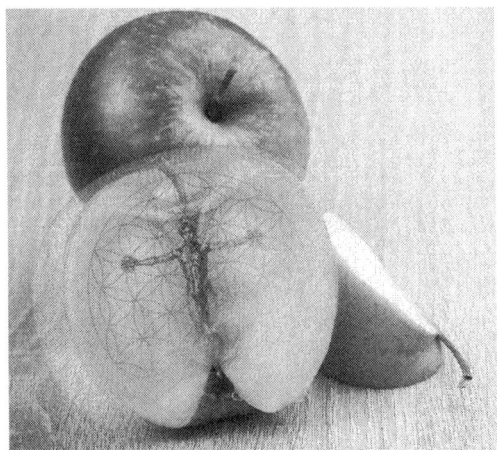

(Fig. 5) The apple-shaped torus field of the human being.

The **serpent** becomes the helical energy of the kundalini.

The **trees** are the *Tree of Life* and the *Tree of Knowledge*.

The **apple** or **fruit** becomes the *apple-shaped torus* energy field flowing and incorporating the pattern of everything (see fig. 5).

Eating from it becomes the act of *consuming, taking in, educating, enlightening* and *awakening by* the female principle instructing serpent stream, Zoe (life).

The metaphors of **looking for** and **finding** in the various accounts represent *perceiving* and *taking possession of* respectively.

Naked means open or exposed.

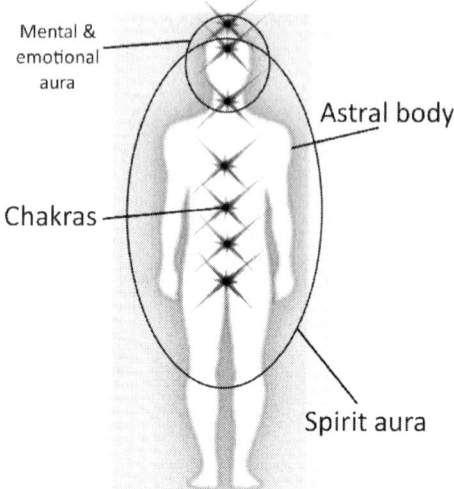

Mental & emotional aura

Astral body

Chakras

Spirit aura

(Fig. 6) Auras. The root entry point is situated between the legs.

The Leaves of the Tree

Before we apply this to the rest of the story, let us also consider what we are told of baptism in *The Exegesis of the Soul* (NHC). The leaves are the spirit part of the human tree, covering the inner workings and giving it its radiant external protective beauty. *15. The womb is on the inside of the body...However, the womb of the soul is external. 16. ...When the womb of the soul, through the will of the Spirit, turns itself inward, it is baptized and cleansed of all exterior pollution that pushed upon it. Like clothing when dirty it is placed into water and washed until all the filth has gone and it becomes clean. And so, the cleaning of the soul is to return it to the originality of its previous nature... That is its baptism.*

When a canopy of leaves and blooms cover a tree, they hide its core structure and give it its radiant, dressed beauty. So, when the demiurge cannot *find* them, it would appear that the empowering element of the sacred trees, their *fig leaves,* are covering over the privy part and root base chakra access point of Adam and Eve. This act on their part represents their attempt to prevent an external controller taking them over or unduly influencing them against their rising enlightenment and freewill.

Find

If you *find* a valuable wallet in the street and pick it up, you possess it by reason of your *finding* it. It belongs to someone else. It is not yours and it never will be unless the true owner decides you should have it. Until that happens, by reason of mischief, you can do what you want with it, that is, you could return it or use it for your own benefit. But if the true owner becomes aware of the theft and stops you by reclaiming their sovereignty over it, then there is very little you can do. After their encounter with the snake, they are now empowered and wiser. Hence,

> 16. *Next* the chief *archon drew close*; and he said, "Adam! Where are you?" - *because* he *did* not *know* what had *taken place.* Adam *replied,* "Your voice [law, word and influence] *became clear to me* and I was *frightened* [by it] because I [realised that I] was naked; [his loin chakra entry point was open] and I hid [under the sacred tree, closing it so it could not be accessed or taken over]."

The next part then becomes,

17. The *archon* said, "*For what reason* did you [close it to me], unless you have [*been educated and instructed by the serpent and*] from the *Tree* [*of Life*] from which I commanded you [*were*] not to [*do*]? And [now] you have [*been enlightened*]!"

18. Adam said, "The woman you *had gifted* me, *gifted* to me [instead] and I ate." And the *conceited archon* cursed *her* [for displaying her intuition, influence, and freethinking].

19. *She* said [to the Chief Archon], "*I* was led astray *by* the [female serpent] the snake, and [then by the reptile] I [was instructed]." They turned to the [serpent, called Zoe] and *damned* its shadowy [soul-like etheric] *manifestation*. [Line missing]. *But the archons were* powerless, [because they did] not *realize* that it was a *being* they themselves had [been trapped into *creating* by Sophia].

So here again the archons are ignorant of the outcome of what they have created, perhaps in the same way a bee does not know the function or science of the complex hive in which it has generated.

From that day, the [enlightening kundalini] snake came to be [under the control] of the archons; until [Jesus] the all-powerful man was to come [to reawaken it once again in the human being].

As Jesus says in the Judas codex, the archons control every human soul. The reawakening of the kundalini in the human represents their single biggest fear of us because it is through this phenomenon that we are connected to the Spirit. Modest research into alien abduction, astral and mind intrusion by archons, both as demons and Ufonauts, reveals that human sovereignty, when asserted over them by fighting back, or invoking what a Natural Spiritualist would call the Power of the Spirit within, causes them to recoil in fear and dread. And for all their imposing stature, reptilians have often been reported to react the same when challenged this way. Archons, in whatever form, live in fear of the human being's potential for true enlightenment and reawakening. So, when a Christian calls out the name of "Christ", or a Muslim calls out "Allah!" or a Hebrew calls out "Yahweh!", it is not important what is shouted, rather it is the solid invocation and calling down of that which is Divine within the human that satisfies the requirements for their salvation in that moment.

As evidenced in the above restored version of the Adam and Eve story, they have fooled us from the outset. They are indeed *alien* and certainly not 'our friends' or 'cosmic family'. Tribal and Native traditions, the world over, are in error when they see them as *brothers* or *guardians*. The NHC is clear on this deception, and in warning against engaging with these lower entity, super elemental life forms.

In this author's first book, *The Psychic & Spiritual Awareness Manual*, p. 17, 'Discerning Auras and their Energies', the spirit aura is described as extending 'furthest from the body, usually half to one third of a metre away. A good indication of this aura's influence can be found when someone invades our space. For instance, we may be on a bus or train or in an office and someone will sit too close. We may or may not feel comfortable with this invasion of our space. If there is a clash in the over lapping field the energies will distort, become resistant and will resemble something akin to the interference on a TV picture. If we are happy with this overlap, then a harmonic resonance may be perceived. By sensing this aura, we get a good indication as to the spiritual nature of the individual. It is said that so-called charismatic people have a strongly developed and widely expanded spirit aura.' (See fig. 6).

As illustrated by Natural Spiritualism, the spiritual aura encloses the sacred organs of the etheric body. Unless it is empowered by the sovereign individual, it cannot offer the desired protection. Suffice it to say, the archons are devoid of this 'spiritual' component part and dread it awakening in the human being.

> 20. They *removed* their [creations] Adam *and Eve* from *their states of Paradise in Gaia Eden*; *because* they *too had* no *spirit component or connection to the Divine within them*, since they too *came under* this curse *of ignorance and damnation. And from then on* [the archons] *hurled* mankind into great distraction [from the pursuit of the Spirit] and into a *lifetime* of toil. [They did this] so that their [version of] mankind might be *distracted* by worldly *things, precluding within them any remaining opportunity of devotion to the holy spirit.*

Holy Spirit means the Divine female principal power of Sophia. For instance, in the (NHC) Gospel of Philip, paragraph 17, Some said that Mary conceived by the Holy Spirit. They are in error. They do not understand what they say. When did a woman ever conceive by a woman? Hence, the Holy Spirit is female. When applied to the orthodox bible and Christian prayer, it can give a very different meaning to things, for example, the sign of the cross; 'In the name of the Father, and of the son, and of the holy ghost.' Also, the oft used phrase, 'Holy Mother of God' – the Mother who comes from God.

Moreover, their removal from their states of Paradise refers to the lowering of their consciousness, or vibration, from Divine to merely etheric and corporeal (merely a thing of the earth). The archons' manipulation of these two constituent parts of the human's tripartite has the effect of placing an aforesaid distraction on that element of the aspiring individual seeking ascension to, and union with, the Spirit from whence they have come. They have sabotaged the human tree and body (matrixes) with deficiencies, causing us to become slaves to weaknesses that can destroy our spirit if left to fester unless brought under our control.

THE CAIN AND ABEL ENIGMA

In the Apocryphon of John, and other sections of the NHC, Cain and Abel are two of the names of the Seven Great Archons of the hebdomad. According to the cynical Manichean idea of Adam and Eve, which classed them both as demons, she gave birth to a son *'deformed in shape and possessing a red complexion, and his name was Cain, the Red Man'.*

Cain's name is of the material plane and means smith, and possibly "to make", hence archon, and so, fashioner and maintainer. Abel's name is purer and associated with the ether and is sometimes translated as "vapor" or "puff of air". Cain is cursed *min-ha-adamah*, from the earth, being the same root as "man" and Adam.

There is a fascinating video lecture given by David Flynn, called The Mars-Earth Connection, where the Cain enigma is addressed by the late researcher. But if you are looking for definitive answers to this part of the creation narrative, then you may be disappointed. There is a poverty of knowledge and understanding in respect of these two figures across all platforms of discussion. This codex does little to shed light on the accepted orthodox version by way of merely replicating it. Wherever it occurs, whether in the Hebrew, Sumerian, or Christian versions, many say it is purely an allegory of brother against brother, victim meets murderer, and so on. A deeper investigation is required. What follows is this author's attempt to bring a greater degree of clarity to the enigma within an NHC framing. The KJV says,

> John, Chapter 3, 11. *For this is the message that ye heard from the beginning, that we should love one another. Not as Cain, who was of that wicked one, and slew his brother. And wherefore slew he him? Because his own works were evil, and his brother's righteous.*

So how could Cain be of that wicked one and Abel not, if they are siblings? Perhaps brother is a mistranslation. If Cain is material and Abel etheric, then Cain, the deceiver and personification of the archon, becomes the embodiment of a warning, namely, that the material world is set up to destroy that which is above it, namely, etheric and spiritual Abel.

> 21. *Now afterwards, she bore Cain, their son; and Cain cultivated the land. Thereupon he knew his wife; again, becoming pregnant, she bore Abel; who was a herdsman of sheep.*

Jesus was the Lamb of God, and like him, we are the lambs. From out of his field, Cain's crops are rejected in favour of the votive (promised, vowed) offerings of Abel, taken from amongst his lambs. So, was he a gatherer of souls 'sacrificed' to the counterfeit God? A field is defined as a cultivated expanse, especially one devoted to a particular crop. Are all these terms metaphors?

> And *flesh* Cain *disposed of* Abel, his brother.

> 22. *God asks Cain to tell him his brother's whereabouts.*

If we accept God as the demiurge, then Cain merely offered flesh, whereas Abel offered souls; something craved by the archons for the spirit they contain. The material world can sometimes consume the soul and that which is in it.

> KJV, Hebrews, Chapter 11, *By faith Abel offered unto God a more excellent sacrifice than Cain, by which he obtained witness that he was righteous, God testifying of his gifts: and by it he being dead yet speaketh* [meaning the truth is known - the spirit speaketh and bears witness to your crime].

And of Cain it says, consistent with the dwelling place of the archons, that he was banished *into* the earth.

> Genesis, {4:11} [The LORD says] And now [art] thou from the earth, which hath opened her mouth to receive thy brother's blood from thy hand;
>
> {4:12} ...a fugitive and a vagabond shalt thou be *in* the earth...
>
> {4:14} [Cain says] Behold, thou hast driven me out this day from the face (surface) of the earth;...and I shall be a fugitive and a vagabond *in* the earth;

NOREA, HER BIRTH AND HER SEED
23-24 (compressed)

Eve, daughter of Sophia, had become pregnant and given birth to a daughter, Norea.

She has several similar names, including Orea and Horaia, all meaning "beautiful". It is thought to derive from a translation of Naamah, a Hebrew name which means "pleasant". The demonised Naamah is called "the younger Lilith". Both Norea and Lilith cry out to the Divine to save them from being raped by demonic intruders.

25. *Then Eve gave birth to Seth through the fatherhood of Adam. She declared that he was "borne" as* "another man through God, to replace Abel." *Again, she became heavy with child and bore* Norea. *And of this* she said, *"He has brought into existence through me one who is a virgin in order to help breed and multiply many new human beings." She is a virgin, and so, untouched by the archons.*

26. *So a fresh seed of mankind was started, and they flourished and became even more advanced.* The *archons* were greatly *distressed* by this and *conspired together, one* with *the* other and *held*, "Come, let us cause a [great] *flood through and by* our hands [so that] all flesh, from *mankind and animal* [alike will be] *destroyed."*

Next, we come to yet another schism in the authority of Yaldabaoth. The first was the loss of his son, Sabaoth to Sophia, recorded in the *Book of Great Secrets* (Ch. 3). In that instance, he had no choice. He faced the superior power. Then later came the rebellious Watchers. But before that occurrence in the timeline, here below, the demiurge goes behind the backs of his creations because he cannot trust them. This would appear to be an early sign of what Eleleth tells Norea at the end of this book, namely, that at the end of the age he will destroy them and then himself.

WHAT WAS THE ARK OF NOAH (AND OF WHAT WAS IT MADE?)

> But when the *Chief Archon* of the *powers learned* of their decision, he *secretly instructed* Noah, [so that he might escape the fate of the world] *to* make [for] *himself* an (*i*) ark *of* (*ii*) wood that *will* not rot and [that he should] hide *himself, his* children, and the *animals* and [all] the birds of heaven, *great and* small *therein* - and *place* it upon Mount (*iii*) Sir."

In Genesis, it is exclusively God, rather than the archons, who decides to destroy the world. {6:13} *And God said unto Noah, The end of all flesh is come before me; for the earth is filled with violence through them; and, behold, I will destroy them with the earth.*

(i) According to etymonline, ark (n.) can be defined as chest or large box, as in the Ark of the Covenant. From the Noachian sense comes the extended meaning, "place of refuge" (17th century). Arcane (adj.) in the Latin can mean "secret, hidden, private, concealed, to close up". In the Greek it can also mean defence. In other words, it has yet to mean boat. That definition seems only to have been applied to the word from the late 15th century.

(ii) Genesis, {6:14} *Make thee an ark of gopher wood; rooms shalt thou make in the ark, and shalt pitch it within and without with pitch.*

The real question is this. Is it wood, metal, or stone? Surprising though it may be, scholars and translators cannot always agree upon the term 'carpenter'. This has often led to firestorm debates between them because the original word is tekton (τέκτων). It is where we get the modern word tech. It means "to make" or "work with". Jesus and Joseph were defined as tektons. Its first meaning is wood, its second is metal, and its last meaning is stone (and oftentimes brick). Joseph the Worker was a tekton in wood, hence carpenter, as was Jesus. But were they? 'Gopher' can be considered a generic term. In the earliest Septuagint bible translation, gopher means square. The homes of Galilea, Samaria and Judea were made almost exclusively from block stone and or brick. They would have ground, chiselled and carved stone before wood, not least because trees were extremely rare. The noted Hebraic scholar, James W. Fleming, is of the opinion that they would have found it very difficult to make a living from carpentry given the scarcity of trees throughout the region. Further, the idea that Jesus and Joseph might in fact have been stonemasons fills many Christians with revulsion.

So, is the ark then made of square stone, wood or metal? What is more, made from 'wood that will not rot...' What wood does not rot? Can we still trust the word rot? What about corrode for metal, or even erode if it is stone? These are all alternatives for rot. And where it says in Genesis '...pitch it within and without with pitch,' what boat has a slanted roof? The bible is also clear that it shall have three storeys and rooms. Does this sound like a boat or is it describing a static, fortified building made of blocks of stone? And of that stone, mud bricks have limited durability against prolonged agitated water saturation. So, stones instead of bricks, if not wood, must it be?

Further, why build a boat that will randomly sail at the behest of violent, stormy seas instead of a solid building positively placed somewhere upon the highest point in the Middle East?

(iii) "...and place it (not sail it to) upon Mount Sir." Many authorities have speculated as to where this might be, and none are of the same mind. Mount Ararat (Genesis, 8:4) in Turkey is the leading contender. Though the OT book says, 'upon the mountains of Ararat' rather than Mount Ararat specifically. But if we take Mount Sir on face value as the true location, can we find any evidence?

Syria is thought to be a derivation of the Hebrew "Sirion" (širyôn), the name the Sidonians gave to Mount Hermon, the highest point in the Middle East. According to Strong's Concordance it is 'a peak of the Lebanon', or Mount Sir. In Chaldean numerology, y is often i and vice-versa, both having the same numeric value. The NHC is concordant with this alphanumeric value for the letters in words, and names used, as well as numbers and values. For instance, Si, Sy are the same as Ci, Cy as in Cydonia. S/C = 3, i/y = 1. The ia suffix means land. Hence, Syr-ia/Sir-ia is the land of Sir, or the land of the Sirs, meaning those who dwell there.

At the expense of Genesis, the Testament of Norea makes a more compelling case for Mount Hermon as the location of the so-called 'ark', especially given its superior elevation, extraordinary and powerful history. The mount itself is 33° North, and there are large, mysterious, ancient altars in the surrounding area that are also perfectly aligned to its summit at 33°.

27. So, does this part represent a breakaway from Yaldabaoth's authority, namely, him confiding in Noah over his archons? Noah is a man under their control. He is the instrument through which their seed will survive the coming destruction. Under no circumstances can he ever allow Norea to enter it and take the risk that she might sabotage the demiurge's plans. With her power and wrath, she blows upon it *'causing it to be consumed by fire'*. 'Blowing' and 'fire' are energies of the soul that come out of the (Holy - *female*) Spirit. This part of the text is a worthy area of discussion. Whatever the nature or form of her power, it is separate from the demiurge and is potent enough to force Noah to make a second ark. *The seeds of organic life contained within the ark (that is, the life) is the imperfect product of the archons.*

28. The *archons convened a meeting with* her, *deciding they would* [pretend to be something they were not and try to lead her into their ways instead of those of the Spirit]. *The demiurge then* said to her *that her* mother, Eve, *had come* to *them.* But Norea *rounded on* them *by reminding them that they* are *'the rulers of the darkness' and that they are* "...*despised and doomed."* She

continued, "And *neither* did you *breed with* my mother; *rather,* it was your *feminine equivalent* you *bred with* [one you yourselves created]. *You are in error because* *I am not your *child*; rather it is from the *realm* above that I *have* come."

*See paragraph 45, *Book of Great Secrets.*

29. *The conceited archon said to her, "Like your mother, Eve, you must give yourself to us." But Norea cried up in a loud voice to the Divine feminine, the Creator of the whole, "Save me from the hands of these archons of wickedness and save me from their clutches - now!"*

30. *The great angel descended from the sky and said to her, "Why are you shouting up to the Creator? Why do you behave so brazenly to the sacred Divine?"*

31. *Norea asked, "Who are you?" The archons of wickedness had now fled.*

32. *"I am Eleleth, wisdom, the great angel whose dwelling is in the company of the Divine feminine."* Then he informed her that *he had* been sent [from above] to speak with *her* and, *"to* save *her* from [falling into] the *hands* of the lawless [ones]." He continued, *"But in order to do that,* I must *instruct* you about your root," [a term which could be widened to also denote the root chakra entry

point].

NOREA'S FIRST-PERSON NARRATION
Eleleth Saves Her from the Archons

33. Now *regarding* that *messenger*, I cannot *find words to describe* his power: his *form* is like *excellent* gold and *clothed in* snow. No, truly, my *lips* cannot *utter the words that might* speak of his power and the *form* of his face!

34. Eleleth, the great *messenger, said* to me. "I am *the one who is knowing*. I am *a giver of light,* one of four [angels and messengers] who *hold place* in the presence of the *boundless, unseen Spirit*. [Why] *are* you *of the belief that* these rulers have any *supremacy* over you? *Not one* of them can *succeed* against *truth's sacred root*. *Because of this,* he [will] *appear* in the *end days*; *resulting in* these archons *being brought under control*. And these archons cannot *spoil* you and that *creation*; *because* your *home* is in *the spirit*, where the virgin *spirit* dwells, who is *over and above* the archons of chaos and [all] their *space*."

35. But I said, "Sir, *instruct* me about the *ability* of these archons - how did they *appear*, and by what *type* of *birth*, and of what *substance*, and who *made* them and their *power*?"

36. *Knowing my concern*, Eleleth *said* to me: "*Inside infinite worlds* dwells *immortal and everlasting Spirit*. Sophia, who is [also]

called Pistis, *wished* to *make* something *independent* [of] her consort; and *what she produced* was a celestial thing [meaning made of shadow and matter]. *There is a* veil [in existence] between the world [that is] above and the *worlds* that are below; and *below that veil, the substance of shadow emerged*; and that shadow *developed into* matter and was [in the void] projected apart. And what she had *brought into being developed into* a *creation* in the matter, *resembling* an aborted foetus [and a thing of poor quality].

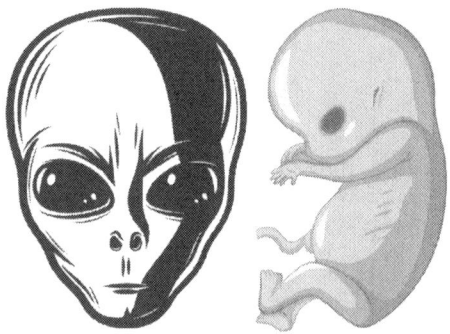

(Fig. 7) Archons of a type in prenatal form.

This is an interesting description because it also tells us that this represents the limit of their physical or aesthetic development. In many ways the archons resemble us up to the mid prenatal stage. The difference being that we progress beyond the womb state through the birth canal and out into the fresh air of the bio-realm, independent of our mother's womb and all that gives us. At this point, the spirit enters the body with the first awakening breath, and we develop into a human being, meaning enlightened spirits possessed of a body, a soul, and a developing, freethinking mind. The foetus in the womb has a body and a developing soul energy but no mind programmed into the hard drive of the brain organ. We are the superior species. We are the superior creation. The problem is the archons are, sometimes, the only ones who seem to know it!

And it *took on an artificial* form *fashioned* out of shadow and *developed into a conceited* beast *similar to an* androgynous lion [because] as I have already *stated*, it was *out of* matter that it *formed*.

37. *When he opened* his eyes, he *perceived an infinite magnitude* of *cosmic* matter; and he *grew to be conceited* [by] *declaring that he alone was God, and that nothing else, apart from him, existed. But in saying* this, he *erred* against the entirety. And [then] a voice *sounded* from above the *dominion* of *supreme authority*, saying, "You are *wrong*, Samael" - which *means*, 'god of the blind'.

38. And he *continued*, "If any *erstwhile* thing exists *prior to* me *then* let me *see it!*" And *at once* Sophia *reached out* her finger and *brought* light into matter; and she *extended* it *downwards into* the *expanse* of chaos. And [then] she *returned back* up to her light [in the 9th heaven]; once *more* darkness [filled...] matter.

39. This *archon*, by [way of his] *androgyny*, *created for* himself a vast, *limitless* s*pace. Then he thought to create* for himself seven *children*, androgynous *and similar to him.* And he *told them*, "I am [the] God of the Entirety."

40. And Zoe (Life), the daughter of Pistis Sophia, *with great clamour* said to him, "You are *wrong*, Sakla!" - for which *another* name is Yaltabaoth. She breathed [life] into *the* face [of all his dominion], and her [living creation] breath became [like] a fiery angel for her; and that *messenger* [greatly] *limited* [the power and influence of] Yaldabaoth *to* [merely that of] *a* [lower] *territory,* Tartarus, [which was situated] *beneath* the *chasm*.

ELELETH DESCRIBES SABAOTH BECOMING THE SUN

41. *Now, as soon as one of his seven children, Sabaoth, witnessed and experienced the power of that fiery angel, he became transformed, and condemned his father of ether and his mother of matter. He could no longer bear to be with them because of his celestial transformation. He now sang songs of tribute and acclaim to Sophia and her child, Zoe, meaning he now resonated, harmonised, and vibrated with them. And Sophia and Zoe captured him and gave him command of the seventh heaven as the sun of the Solar System, beneath the veil that sits between the above and the below. And he is called 'Generator of the celestial forces, Sabaoth', because he is over all the forces of chaos, because Sophia established*

him there.

TRANSFORMATION OF THE CELESTIAL SKY

42. *After this had transpired,* he *created for* himself *an enormous* four-faced chariot of cherubim [the four constellations of the ogdoad that remain fixed to the naked eye], and *an infinite number of* angels to act as *servants, as well as* harps and lyres [symbolising sacred life resonances and harmonies]. And Sophia *sat* her daughter, Zoe, *on* his right to *instruct* him *concerning all* the things that *are* in the eighth *heavenly* [ogdoad -Milky Way]; and the *child* of *rage* she *positioned on* his left. *Ever since* that day, his right [half] *is named* 'life'; and [his] left [half] has come to *signify* the *wickedness* of the *world* of *fixed control* above. *All this* was before your time [and the creation of the Anthropos] that they came into *existence.* (Fig. 9).

43. Now when Yaldabaoth saw *his child, Sabaoth, raised up* in *all his brilliance,* he envied him; and *that* envy *developed into* an androgynous *creation* [because being made of matter and ether it was neither male or female], and *so began* envy. And envy *produced Death* [meaning mortality]; and [the demiurge of] death *produced* his *children* and gave each of them *dominion over their sphere*; and all the *spheres* of chaos *grew to be filled with* their multitudes. *And* it was by the *determination* of the *Creator* of the *Entirety* that they *were made - in accordance with* the *model* of all the

things *on high* - so that the [principal void of] chaos might be *brought into one with the light.*

44. "There, I have *educated* you about the *way* of the rulers; and [also] the matter *within* which it was *made*; and their *father*; and their universe."

45. Then I *asked*, "*Lord*, how much longer?"

46. "You *and all* your *children*, *come* from the *pre-existing parent* [who came] from *on high* [and] out of the *everlasting* light, their souls *appear*. *Therefore,* the archons *are unable to come near* them *for the reason* of the spirit of truth *that lives* within them; and all [those humans] who *seek this truth for themselves shall have eternal life while the rest around them shall die*. Still, that *seeded part* will not *be recognised just* now. *Rather, at the end of the* three *Ages shall* it *become* known, and it has *liberated* them from the *captivity* of the *archons'* error."

47. I [then] *asked*, "*Lord* [Eleleth], *do* I also *come* from their matter?"

48. He said to me, "*In anticipation of* the *event* when the true man [shall come], *contained* within a *fashioned figure*, [and] *makes known* the existence of the *Spirit of Truth*, which the *Christos* has sent.

49. Then he *shall tutor* them *on the subject of all things*, and *they* will *be anointed* with

the *balm* of *immortal* life [that was] given [to] him from the *Creator of the Entirety.*

50. *Then will come liberation from blind thought. They will tread upon the Death that is the archons. They will rise into the infinite light where they have their place.*

The next passage, 51, says the archons will be forced to give-up, surrender their age of control, and their created retinue (angels and demons) will cry bitter tears at their end.

The next passage, 52, says that

every child that is of the light will be justly joined to the truth and from whence they came in union with the God of the Entirety and the holy spirit. And in that unity, they will say, as with one voice,

"The (1) *Father's* truth is *law*, and the (2) son *reigns* over the entirety", and *over all to* the *end* of ages, (3) *"Sophia - Sophia - Sophia! (4) So be it!"*

Or 'In the name of the (1) Father, and of the (2) son, and of the (3) holy spirit. (4) Amen.'

CHAPTER THREE

MAJOR ARCANA:
THE GREAT BOOK OF SECRETS
REVEALED

A RETRANSLATION INTO PLAINER ENGLISH
OF THE BOOK
ON THE ORIGIN OF THE WORLD

For reference, what follows is based on the translations of Hans-Gebhard Bethge and Bentley Layton.

THE THREE AGES OF THIS CODEX

1st Age is the age of the Creator of the Entirety – Big (Absolute) God.

2nd Age is the creation of a principal void of space, or vast chasm called 'chaos'.

3rd Age is our current age, the one we live in, namely, that of the creation of matter and ether within the void.

The term chaos for the universe can be a distraction because it can carry with it all manner of anarchic connotations implying states of disorder and confusion. Within physics, it is the quality of a complicated structure whose actions are so unpredictable as to appear random to the observer. It is interesting to note that the scientific elites gave the name Chaos (Khaos) to the formless matter thought to have existed before the creation of the universe. According to this book, the universe we see is contained merely within a part of the void of chaos, meaning outer space is not infinite but a finite thing.

Note: [] Square brackets in the following represent author comment, expansion, and paraphrase within the texts.

Italics represent author retranslations.

A Glossary of Terms used in the NHC can be found at the rear of this book.

> *(1) Everyone, including the gods* [archons] *of the earth and humankind, assert nothing had life before chaos* [the universe], *I shall reveal to them their error, for they are not familiar with the beginning of chaos or its cause.* Here is the *revealing*.

From the off, this bold text sets down a challenge to Genesis which cites the creation of the world by Almighty God as the true beginning to all things. In his place we are offered a demiurge called Yaldabaoth, meaning the Child of Chaos, whom the NHC authors have defined as the counterfeit god and not the one true Creator of the Entirety. This is usually the point at which many slam the book shut and go back to the relative safety of their accepted paradigm.

Next, the Creator generates super gods or principal classes of aeons who are generally considered to exist in pairs though, as with Sophia, can act independent of one another. In the Entire scheme of things, Christos, the divine (heavenly) masculine god and Sophia, the divine feminine goddess, are lower aeons, androgynous - though for the purposes of understanding, favour male and female polarities respectively, or the differences between them. They are also responsible for creating all the life that exists within the celestial heavens.

(2) *It is all too easy and convenient for people to say that the void of chaos is a type of darkness!* [Ether]. *But in truth it came from a shadow* [principal breath or soul energy] *that was cast out* [breathed] *by the Creator who has had life since the beginning.*

THE PRE-EXISTING GOD

It is likewise, plain that it had life earlier than when the void of chaos came into being, and that the darkness came after the first creation. We shall concern ourselves [only] with *its evidence*; and *also*, with the *earliest creation* from which [the void of] chaos was projected. *So shall* the *truth of the world and the heavens become clear* [to you].

*'Truth of the World and the Heavens' would also be a fitting alternative title for this codex.

DEFINING 'PISTIS' AND 'WISDOM' IN THIS TEXT

Before we go any further, and in order to better understand what unfolds along the creation timeline, we first need to define Pistis and wisdom as uniquely expressed within the contexts of the NHC. In other words, what these things are and how they are used to bring about the subsequent order and creations.

PISTIS

Pistis Sophia, meaning wisdom, so called to denote a wise creator/generator goddess, was formed, or emanated through and by the hand of something very special and supreme in (and above) our universe - that is to say, a power known as Pistis which can only come from one source, that of the Creator. And when expressed through a freethinking, enlightened, enterprising aeon such as Sophia, that exceptional and singular thing becomes the instrument. It is the name given to the personification, (accepted to be the) generation and manifestation of the Way (meaning the Will, control, and authority) of the Creator of the Entirety; the overall supreme controller (so defined).

Other words with the *pis* stem are piscine and Pisces. It means water, or of the water. Then we have Jesus Christ symbolised by the ichthys. It is defined in terms of its emergence as a secret symbol for early persecuted Christians, where two arches intersect and resemble a fish. But it is more than that. The binding together of Pistis power and the revealing and healing ministry of Jesus make it clear why it was chosen. This latter fact is, unsurprisingly, never discussed in academia or churchianity, where the larger emphasis is placed upon the habits of church ceremonies and institutional traditions, rather than on the spiritual teachings of Jesus.

WISDOM
Wisdom and wise are words that, in the time of the authorship of the texts, often meant something quite different. Wisdom in the NHC should not be taken to mean philosophy or experience. Most, if not all NHC readers and scholars define it in terms of gnosis, power, and law. But it may more accurately be thought of as the ability of an aeon or a god to create; to wit, a type of wisdom-*wizardry.* For example, the texts describe the reptilian 'Beast' in the garden as the 'wisest of all the beasts', not least because he was the best made. Therefore, wisdom should be taken to mean that which is created, or made, through and by the hand of the aforementioned powers. This is why the demiurge (counterfeit god) can sometimes be said to also have wisdom.

But this book tells us it is important to remember that Pistis (Sophia) did not come about until the appearance of the so-called seventy-two 'immortal beings' (and their Spirit realms encoded in the sacred Tree of Life) who had developed out of the same professed 'infinite', meaning principal void of chaos. So, it would be fair to assume that Pistis phenomena are unique to the aeons, or that which works through them, and hence extended to that which they create.

PISTIS SOPHIA, THE TRANSFORMING AEON
It is speculated by certain scholars, especially those outside the mainstream, that she somehow morphed

into the material earth. But this belief makes little sense to true students and teachers of psychic and spiritual science for two main reasons. Firstly, there is the maxim, *that which is of the spirit is spirit, and that which is of matter is matter.*

This law means Sophia could *not,* as it were, transform downwards into something of a lesser order, or become something else altogether, any more than we can morph into the lower order material things we make and manufacture for ourselves. Put simply, if a woman makes a garment, she puts something of herself into its creation and design, but she is *not* the garment, and neither can she become it! These notions are distractions which can lead the enquirer down blind alleys and rabbit warrens filled with nonsense and have been demonstrated time and again to be the product of poor-quality thinking. And secondly, not least because, this codex states Earth does not yet exist and when it does it will be made by the, soon to be created, self-declared god to become 'his footstool'. And so, we come to –

THE BIRTH OF SOPHIA

(3) *Once* the *eternal living aeons* had *fully grown and organised themselves within their natural order in* [that part of] the infinite [void of chaos which resembled a type of womb], a *replication* then *radiated* from Pistis [in the form of a female power]. [She] *was given the name* Sophia. *Of her own accord, she turned herself into* a *created phenomenon similar to* the *primordial* creation light. And *at once* her will [demonstrated and displayed] itself as a *reproduction* of heaven and *was of a size*

beyond imagination. It *occupied the space between the high spirit planes of* the immortal beings and [the lower planes of] *shadow, matter, and the celestial heavens. And by doing so, she created* a veil [which would] *divide* [yet to be created] mankind from *all that is* above.

WATERS

The 'waters' that fill the void of chaos are, for the first time, defined once and for all by the NHC as the flow and fluid vortices incorporating all the dynamics of the cosmic womb that surround and connect the Divine creations that exist within it, i.e., the aeons. Spirits, demons, ETs, and archons also move through it unobstructed like fishes through water.

(4) *The immortal, everlasting spirit World of Truth is not composed of* matter, *only* light. *However,* its *outer part* is [made of a soul-like substance called] darkness. *And* from [this] *a power materialised* [which came to] *rule* over [and dominate] *that* darkness. And the *power*s [Sophia and Christos] *who appeared after those who first appeared* (the sacred seventy-two of the Creator's womb), *gave* the shadow [a title - that of] 'the [realm of] *endless* chaos', *out of which all manner* of deity *emerged* [and flourished] *mutually in the midst* of *that whole territory*. So [let it be clear] that shadow [soul] *substance came after* the first [spirit] *creation*. It was *within* the abyss [or lower part of this ether] that *matter*

emerged, drawing [its existence and materialisation] from the *abovementioned* Pistis [power and phenomena].

YALTABAOTH AS SHADOW

(5) Then shadow *detected* [by instinct] *a presence more powerful and greater* than *itself,* and [found itself] *experiencing* [a desire to have as its own, something that belonged to that mightier power; a touch of something which it did not itself possess or by which it was so gifted. And by reason of its failure to acquire its special light and spirit, a type of 'envy' then followed].

We are talking here about the formation of our immediate universe and its counterpart in the etheric with Yaltabaoth. Shadow/ether is a lesser substance to that of the spirit from which the soul is made. The plane it formed is that of the etheric astral and can be divided into higher and lower (for ease of understanding) and should not be confused with the Spirit World, heaven or the true afterlife.

In the following passage Yaltabaoth's growth is characterised by the negative traits of jealousy and envy.

Without aid it (Yaltabaoth) *became* pregnant, [so hence that part of the shadow realm came to be womblike and] it *immediately brought about* *envy. *From that moment*, the *perception and trait* of *possessiveness* amongst all the *everlasting*

71

realms and their *domains* has been [clear and] *evident*.

*Envy, on the part of the negative, or creation error, is a very important territorial theme in these codices and requires further study and understanding on the part of the student. In short, it means to ultimately destroy that which it cannot have for itself. This characteristic shall become clear as we progress through the timeline.

THE CREATION OF MATTER OUT OF SHADOW

Now as for that *enviousness*, it *turned out* to be [a thing of Death] an abortion [existing] *with no* spirit [part] in it. *As* a shadow, *its life* came into [being] *within* a *cosmic fluid material*. Then the *fluid residue* that *developed* out of the *ether* was *discharged* into *a* [certain] *area* of chaos. Since *then*, a *cosmic material of fluidity* has been clear and *evident*. And what [was contained] within it *descended* [and] *poured* away *to become* visible in [the universe]: *just as when* a woman *births* a child – all [of] her *waters stream* out; [and in this same way, the substance of] matter *materialised from* shadow, [a product born of the embryonic waters of that womb] and was [in the void] projected. *But* it did not [extend beyond the outer limits of] chaos; rather, matter *stayed within* [the realm of] chaos, *becoming an integral* part of it (perhaps affirming the material universe is really a finite one).

THE CREATION OF THE DEMIURGE:

(6) [Once this happened], Pistis [the personification of the Creator's energy] *moved* [unseen] *towards the substance of* matter *and materialised in every part of it in* chaos. *It had been ejected* [like] an aborted foetus [would be ejected] - *given that* there was no spirit in it [for it was a thing of Death]. The void of chaos *in* [which finite matter exists] was infinite. Now when Pistis *witnessed the end resulting product of* her *imperfection, it unsettled her greatly.* And *that unsettlement* appeared, as a *fearful creation*; [and] it *hastily came* to her in the [void of] chaos [attracted by her light and corresponding life energy]. She *connected* to it and *streamed* [her] *life* [force, but not her spirit light], into *it* in the abyss *that sits beneath* all the heavens [thereby creating what the texts call the Lower Sophia version of herself].

*Fearful appears in the English translation but is yet another word chosen by scholars for its multiple meanings. So, in this context does it mean (a) *full of fear,* (b) *monstrous and likely to cause fear,* (c) *immense* or perhaps all three? The first would indicate Sophia felt motherly towards him and sought to bring him comfort. The second would indicate she had inadvertently birthed a monster. And the latter would indicate scale and hence the size of the problem.

As we shall explore a little further on, (perhaps) because she acted alone - a virgin birth - this caused the anomalous creation of a demiurge, something which had every possibility of not occurring had she acted in partnership with her male counterpart, or 'husband' of 'the bridal chamber', the 'Christos' aeon. This codex reveals the secret that the human being is created as the Divine Feminine solution to the problem of Yaltabaoth.

In its original translation into English, the following passage is very difficult to interpret; hence it is simply re-written here in order to keep its message and meaning intact.

(7) *So Pistis Sophia, in keeping with the pattern of the higher things and her freethinking, enterprising nature, brought about the formation, and a subsequent creation* [in the substance of the cosmic media] *of a demiurge* [meaning artisan] *who would become the controller and fashioner of this aspect of chaos. He was a low male energy but made in her image to serve* [under] *Pistis, to do her apparent bidding and fully realise her image, dream, and idea in that place. And that creation, as she intended, turned out to be a princely ruler, grown from the media of shadow and matter, resembling an androgynous lion and, like a lion, was chief of his domain and completely ignorant of his origins. And Sophia perceived him deep in the cosmic waters moving freely and without impediment. She connected to him like a mother connecting to her new-born child. And she whispered to him, "Child of chaos, whom I have birthed, come to me."*

So, in this area of darkness, an intelligent force made of a special substance moved freely with no spirit in it. It was a complex living entity that swam about like an abysmal fish of the ocean floor, devoid of sight and, therefore, unable to perceive light. But it would appear to have had the wherewithal to know there was something greater than itself in the void.

> (8) *From* that *moment*, [the Entire God's formulation and plan] *became clear and it extended to* the gods, angels, and mankind. And what *materialised* as a *consequence* of *this principle*, the gods [forces] and the angels [energies] and [future] mankind [thus] *completed* [meaning all is planned and in the order of things]. Now *regarding* the ruler, Yaltabaoth, he is *unaware* of the *power* of Pistis: he did not *perceive* her [full] face, rather he *perceived through* the [cosmic] water the *image* that *communicated and connected to* him [and not her full aspect]. And *for the reason* of that voice [meaning word, meaning God], he called himself *'Yaldabaoth'. But 'Ariael' (meaning the Archangel of Principalities) is *how the high ones referred to* him, *because of his similarity to* a lion. Now *once his power and dominion* over matter had *been accomplished*, Pistis Sophia *departed* up to her light [in the 9th Heaven that sits above the Milky Way].

*Change of spelling.

According to the forethought of Pistis Sophia, he was organised within the realm like a balancing elemental force for the production and maintenance of the shadow and the material planes, accomplishing a type of equilibrium in the shadow and matter as a counter to the generated, or created, 'error', for that is how she left it. Ariael is variously accepted as the lion of God, and principalities refers to devolved territories ruled over by lesser gods and goddesses (archons).

This becomes an important point in what is recorded next in the Old Testament book of Isaiah 66: 1 concerning the Abrahamic 'God Almighty' and his 'creating the earth as his footstool'.

THE DEMIURGE CREATES THE EARTH

(9) When the ruler saw *the enormity and extent, not only of himself but also of his realm* - and *perceived nothing else other than himself within that fluidity* and darkness – *it led him to conclude that* he alone existed *throughout*. His [personification and will; his formulation and plan] was [then] *accomplished*. It *materialised like* a spirit [waveform] *going back and forth over* the [etheric] waters. And when that spirit *became visible* [as a force for creation], the ruler set apart the *fluid* substance. And what was *waterless* [meaning solid matter] was *separated* into *a different* place. And *out of* matter, he *fashioned* himself a *dwelling*, and he *named* it 'heaven'. And from matter, the ruler [also] *fashioned* a footstool, and *named* it [the] *'earth'*.

THE DEMIURGE CREATES THE ARCHONS

(10) *After that, in accordance, he created* [for himself] *three* [that where] *androgyne,* [who were sons of their father], 'consistent with his nature', meaning similar to himself.

The first he called Yao (sometimes spelt Iao and linked to the Egyptian male aeon, Osiris)
The second he called Eloai
The third he called Astaphaios.

(11) Seven [Great androgynous Archons then] appeared in chaos. They have *male and female* names. The *female* name is,

(Representing *'week'*) Pronoia
(Forethought) Sambathas.
(*Lordship*) his son is called Yao.
(*Armies*) Sabaoth: his feminine name is Deity.
Adonaios: his feminine name is Kingship.
Elaios: his feminine name is Jealousy.
Oraios: his feminine name is Wealth.
Astaphaios: his feminine name is Sophia (here meaning negative wisdom, mischief, barrier).

So named are the seven *powers* of the seven *spheres* of chaos [hebdomad or soon-to-be-formed solar system], **imbalanced with energies of* (predominantly) *male and female* [exact and] consistent with the *eternal prototype* that *had life* before them, *through and by* the *will* of Pistis…

*Throughout the timeline of the NHC she sometimes appears ineffectual to many observers. To them, it would seem, she has birthed a deficient, bastard son because she herself was deficient by virtue of creating him without her equal male counterpart. Some commentators have speculated this is why the archons will grow to become predatory, parasitic, demented entities.

In human terms, a tiny organism can infect a whole body. And in the same way a human can take time to fight an infection or dis-ease, conceivably so too Sophia. Is her single energy polarity too weak compared to that which would have come about had she made her creation from the combined power of the two polarities? What we are told in the codices is she acted alone. Had her creation been born of a union from the start then perhaps the problem would never have arisen and so hence, neither would we exist! But we must never lose sight of the fact that all these things are in accordance with the God of the Entirety.

The line continues -

> ...so that the *image and reproduction* of *that which* reigned *before would do so thereafter* to the end [of our current 3rd Age]. You will find the (i) effect of these *designations* and the *power* of the *masculine* entities in the *Archangelic (Book) of the Prophet Moses*, and the *designations* of the female *ones* in the first (ii) *Book/Account of Noraia.*

(i) The *effect* one might look for here is the strong but invisible bond, or psychic web, that links all life together through the shared qualities and traits of the soul, or psyche of the human, as well as from where they originate. In the same way good spiritual beings can inspire us to be likewise the same, so too can harmful ones. In respect of the latter, the Book also contains shielding, exorcistic invocations to ward off archon powers and intrusions.

(ii) (Author opinion) True name for *Hypostasis of the Archons* codex, Chapter Three.

Before we venture further, it is worth reminding ourselves that the heavens of the material plane, as seen by the naked eye from the surface of the earth, are made up of the planets of the hebdomad (solar system) and the fixed dome of stars (Milky Way) or Ogdoad.

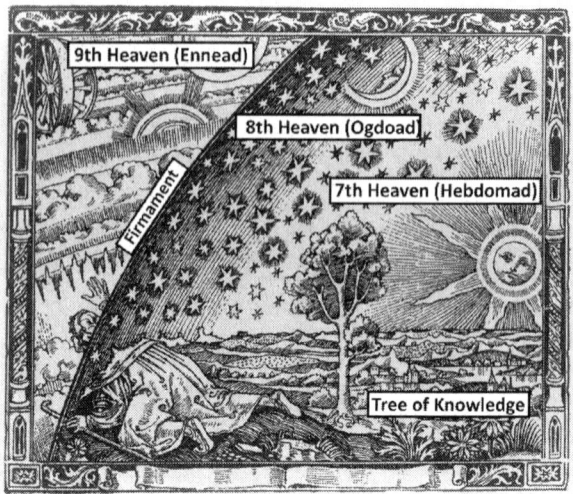

(Fig. 8) Flammarion epitomises the quest for knowledge.

The following passage suggest strongly that a Great Archon dwells within each of the spheres of our solar system. We must also remember that the material world has an etheric counterpart.

THE DEMIURGE CREATES THE FORERUNNER OF THE SOLAR SYSTEM

(12) Now the *chief* parent Yaltabaoth, *because he now exercised control over these Great Archons, fashioned for* each of his *children a* heaven [sphere or planet] *of their own* through [the power of his formulation and plan] - *fashioned* them *beautifully*, as dwelling places - and in each *one* he *fashioned* great glories, *seven excellent spheres.*

Their astrological, *kabbalistic ascensions, and *progressions* [meaning the science of God] are variously described in a list of exemplary things representing the very best of which he is capable. These [celestial] creations [and their movements] *are,*

Thrones [meaning that upon which he sits when entering an astrological house of which he is a ruler]
Mansions (see Glossary) [also meaning astrological houses]
Temples [meaning astrological units, configurations, and eclipses such as those recorded in Egyptian and Vedic astrology, and also pictured on the disk of the sacred sky Temple of Hathor,]
Chariots [meaning vehicles facilitating and accompanying their movements across the sky]
Virgin spirits [meaning, singular and either male or female without intercourse or entwinement] up to an *unseen* one [Sophia] and their glories [and] each one *contains the following* [things] *within* his *sphere* [a vertically integrated hierarchy of spiritual entities described as], *powerful* **armies of gods, lords, angels, archangels, countless myriads** - so that [these intelligent forces which translate as laws, energies of the spirit, etheric and natural levels alike] might *work* [according to his order of things]. The account of [*all*] these *things* you will find *strictly defined* in the

first *Account of Oraia* [aka Orea, Noraia, Noria] (Chapter Three).

(Fig. 9) The celestial chariots draw the heavenly bodies across the sky under number seven of the hebdomad/solar system.

So, now there is a system of sorts, balanced and complete. Then a cosmic and etheric upheaval takes place. To better understand what happens next, it might help to become acquainted with at least three key theories of celestial upheaval contained within the mythological, historic, and scientific record, though others are available.

THE SOLAR SYSTEM IS TORN

The following items are discussed in some detail in Chapter Four.

(a) Velikovsky's *Worlds in Collision* (1950).
(b) *The Electric Universe Theory* and *The Thunderbolts Project* (David Talbott and Wallace Thornhill).
(c) Carlos Muñoz Ferrada's (1909-2001) study and warning of *'Hercolubus'*.

Note: Many find the following a little difficult to comprehend.

> (13) And they were *made* from this heaven
> *all the way up to* the sixth heaven, *explicitly*
> that of [the lower] *Sophia.

*(First mentioned in the last line of paragraph 6, *The Creation of the Demiurge*). Do not be confused by that statement (and in what follows), i.e., that Sophia is, somehow, suddenly the daughter of Yaldabaoth! In Valentinian Gnosticism, there is an Upper and Lower Sophia (Wisdom). For ease of understanding (in this instance) she is the demiurge's instrument, and her name should be changed to that of *Pronoia, daughter of Yaldabaoth*. She is his version of the single helix, serpent life stream. Remember, with the NHC all is reflection and replication.

The following passage is very difficult to decipher, or understand in its original form, so it is here re-translated into plain English to the best of the author's understanding and ability.

THE SOPHIA OF THE LOWER PLANE

The solar system and the earth were devastated by the *troublemaker that was beneath them all. And the six planets shook violently, not least because the high angelic architects of the universe knew who it was that had caused the devastation on the plane beneath them. And when Pistis saw the terrible result of this celestial disturbance, she wielded her power and bound him up and cast him down into Tartarus, that place which is the lower nightmare level of the astral realm. From then on, the six planets and the moon by the side of its earth, strengthened and secured itself through the power of the negative Sophia (Pronoia), meaning she accomplished this through and by the hand of her father, Yaldabaoth, that is to say, she who is below them all.

*Hercolubus was described by Carlos Muñoz Ferrada as 'the destroyer from below' because it enters the solar system beneath the ecliptic plane of the spheres and is only visible from Antarctica.

(14) *And so, a new celestial order was established,* causing the prime parent, *Yaldabaoth, to become impudent.* He was *so pleased to see* the army of [archon] angels *that were generated through and by this change.* And *he was given respect and consent by them* all [and they demonstrated it by obeying his powers of cosmic and

etheric influence]. And for his [own] part, he was *elated* and *became consistent in his control* [and mastery]. [Then] he *said* to them, "I *am without* need of anyone. I *am the one* who *is* God. There is no other *in existence* apart from me" [No other did he detect in the void]. *By speaking these words*, he *sinned and greatly insulted* all the *eternal ones* who *answer to the Creator.* And [so] *those* [that were above him decided to] *put things in order* given his *lawbreaking.*

(15) When Pistis *witnessed* the *conceit* [and error] of the chief *archon*, she *became filled with wrath*. She was *imperceptible* [to him]. She *replied*, "You are *wrong*, Samael," (*which means* god *of the* blind). "There is an *eternal* man of light [my consort, the Christos] who has *had life* before you, and *whose* [personification] will appear among your [yet to be created anthropoid] *modelled forms [in a figure called 'Jesus' who will be the 'perfect human' personification of him and] he will *pound* you *with contempt*, just as *a potter pounds clay."

*Here Sophia reveals to the archons the entire template of the human being (Anthropos), thereby fooling them into creating something that will ultimately destroy them by way of their envious replication of it.

THE BEGINNING OF THE DESTRUCTION OF THE ARCHONS.
Sophia Reveals to them their End!

"And you will *go down* to your mother [that birthed you, that is], the abyss [of shadow and matter], *together* with those [spirits of error and archon children] *ruled by* you. For at the *accomplishment* of [all] your [many] works, the *whole imperfection* that has become visible [meaning Pistis Sophia's transformation of his system of planets] out of the [One] truth will be *eliminated*, and it will *end as if it had* never *existed* [at all]". Saying this, *Sophia* revealed *the* greatness of her *forethought* [and plan] in the [cosmic] *fluid* [as an image of the coming Christos-like Anthropos]. And [in] so doing, she [then] withdrew *upwards into* her light [in the 9th heaven].

SABAOTH BECOMES OUR SUN
The Lucifer Enigma Made Clear

The texts reveal that Lucifer is not Satan. They are two completely different *things*. The former is a powerful celestial force and the latter, a powerful reptilian entity. Orthodox Christian tradition created the perceived confusion when it converted the word *lucifer* into a proper noun, *Lucifer,* to describe Satan before his fall from grace. The Latin Vulgate name, *Lucifer* is a version of the Hebrew word *hêlêl* or *heylel* found in Isiah 14:12. Its similarity to the word *hell* and *Helios* (sun) meaning fire or flame, and its European variants, cannot be ignored. Then there is *hêlêl ben šāḥar*, defined by the King James Version as *"O Lucifer, son* [sun] *of the morning!"* and by others as *'morning star, son* [sun] *of the dawn'.*

Lucifer appears only once in both the Hebrew text and KJV. It is variously translated in Strong's Concordance as *'Venus', 'morning star', 'shining one', 'light bringing'* or *'bringer of dawn'.* Post KJV translations of the bible use one of the aforementioned terms in place of *Lucifer.* According to the Canaanites, a lesser god called *Helel,* attempted to overthrow *El* (another name for the Old Testament God) whose dwelling was upon a mountain to the north. Another word for north is top. So, *north* can be translated as the crown chakra of the human trees of life and knowledge that are formed within us, thereby preventing a connection to the Divine source.

The authors of the NHC *knew,* without a doubt, that Venus was a planet of the hebdomad and not a star of the ogdoad, not least because it moved independently of the dome of the fixed stars. So now we can interpret Sabaoth, son of Yaldabaoth as Lucifer and Sun. Pronoia, who is the daughter of Yaldabaoth, is the lower version of Sophia's daughter, Zoe (life). She is responsible for creating *his* version of *life.* Pronoia's worth will become even clearer below. But for now, it is enough to know her name also means the subdivision of a *week* or *seven days.* The two are entwined together. The significance of this can be found in those parts of the texts where Sabaoth also means 7th day or Sunday, repose (or rest) and perhaps his name is the true origin of the term Sabbath, day of rest.

The lion-faced demiurge is also known as 'Leo', who, according to Vedic and Equal House astrology that are an influence in the NHC, or vice versa, *'thinks* he rules the world'. In the Sibylline Oracles' recording of the battle of the skies, 'Lucifer fought mounted on the back of Leo [the lion-faced Yaldabaoth]' (line 517). The Age of Leo, the fire sign, occurred circa 12,500 BC in concordance with Atlantis.

Lucifer, like Satan, opposes the demiurge, challenging him and questioning his authority. So, by accepting his transformation into the bright, shining sun of the solar system, he now finds himself completely at odds with his father, Yaldabaoth. And as this text points out, he is now superior to his father. Jesus is recorded in the *Sophia Wisdom of Jesus Christ* acknowledging the same paradox (at the same point in the narrative) where the powers of the father differ from those of the son, and how the son becomes greater than the one that fathered him.

Paragraph 22. Jesus says, *"With regard to eternity*, they [Yaldabaoth and Sabaoth] are indeed *one and the same* [meaning their longevity will only last as long as the 3rd Age]. (But) in respect to power, they are *not the same*, like the *distinction* between father and son."

SABAOTH BECOMES LUCIFER, "THE 1ST ADAM"

There are three types of Adam in the NHC. Here is the first.

> (16) *Once* Yaldabaoth's *son*, [he of the name] Sabaoth *perceived and* [experienced the resonances and power] of [Divine] Pistis, he [replied in harmony, thereby putting him out of tune with Yaldabaoth] at the *formulation and execution* of Pistis; and he [replied in harmony to] her because she had **made known to* them *all the things of* the

immortal man and his *spirit* [part, as well as Sabaoth's potential to host and help generate types of life as our sun].

*Sophia connected to him, and he responded to her superior aeon touch. No longer did he respond to lesser Yaldabaoth. Instead, he became the instrument through which she could progress her Divine Mission Plan.

Then Pistis Sophia, *with a* finger *of* her hand, *pointed* [an aeon transformation] and [by doing so] *transferred to* him *a quantity of* [creation] light from her light *that challenged the darkness* of his father. [Then] Sabaoth, *once illumined, became invested with immense power* [acting] *in opposition to each of* the [cosmic] forces of chaos [greater than those of his father]. *From that day to this he is known as* "Lord of the Forces" [becoming the sun of the solar system, Lucifer, bringer of light].

(17) [He now shone brightly with light and power]. *He had turned into an opposite of* his father [who was of] the darkness, and [she who was of the] *chasm*, his mother. And [he] *despised* his sister [Pronoia] too. [And he turned against] *every work* of the *demiurge that moved back and forth over* the [cosmic] waters. And *for the reason of* his light, all the *archons* of chaos were *envious* of him [in the same way Yaldabaoth had envied in the chaos that of which he too was deficient]. And *in being*

so disturbed [by him,] they [reacted by] *engaging in* a *mighty* war in the seven *spheres* [resulting in a cosmic disorder and upheaval that lasted until a new order could be established in the solar system].

MOVEMENTS AND THE NEW CELESTIAL SUN

When Pistis Sophia had *witnessed* the war [meaning all manner of disturbance and phenomena between the spheres], she dispatched seven [celestial] archangels [for aid and assistance] to Sabaoth from [out of] her light [to counter Yaldabaoth]. They *snared* him [and lifted him] up [from being a planetary sphere] to the seventh heaven, [thereby making him a sun, and resting (or 'reposing' him) in that position]. They *rose* before him *like followers. In addition*, she *dispatched* [to] him three more archangels [for aid] *to begin his monarchy from his abode* above the twelve [astrological houses] gods of chaos, *a monarchy that would reign* [in the sky] over *them all* [the sun].

(18) Now when Sabaoth [became a living sun, he altered his position by] *taking* up *rest* in *a* place of [peace and equilibrium] *as a reward* for his *change and transformation, whereupon* Pistis *then gifted* him her daughter Zoe [or aeon serpent stream, so that he became bestowed with all the things of a living sun], together with great *cosmic powers and influences*, so that she might [now] *connect* him *with regard to everything* that *lives* in the

[firmament of the] eighth heaven [for with that place he now shared a unifying harmony]. And as he [was now endowed with greater] *power and influence* [than his father, the first thing] he *created* [for] himself [was an astrological] mansion. It is *vast*, *great*, seven times *the immensity of* all [that are] in the seven heavens.

The sun we see today is the portal through which the beam of divine life energy, the Eve ray, is focussed.

BUILDING THE CONSTELLATIONS AND ASTROLOGICAL HOUSES

The next passage reveals a celestial wheel which sets down the new order of things around him and how he connects himself as one above the seven (See fig.4).

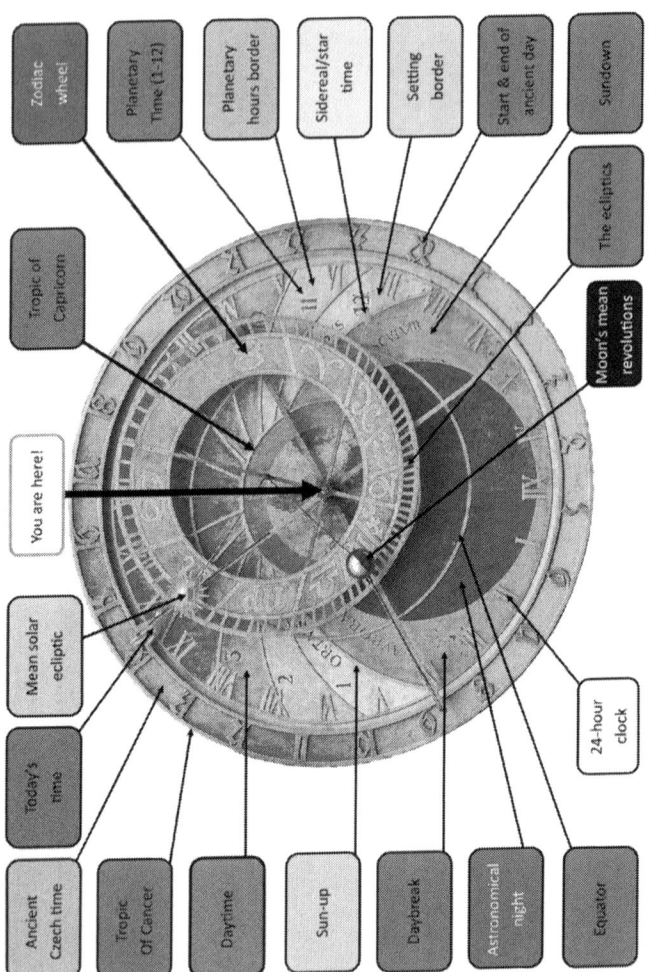

Zodiac wheel

Planetary Time (1-12)

Planetary hours border

Sidereal/star time

Setting border

Start & end of ancient day

Sundown

Tropic of Capricorn

The ecliptics

Moon's mean revolutions

You are here!

Mean solar ecliptic

Today's time

24-hour clock

Ancient Czech time

Tropic Of Cancer

Daytime

Sun-up

Daybreak

Astronomical night

Equator

(Fig. 10) The Prague Astronomical Clock is a wonderful example of how Pistis Sophia's orbital, celestial, and zodiacal mechanics work.

(19) And before his mansion [astrological house] he created a throne [astrological term for a planet which sits on its throne when in a sign of which it is a ruler], which was

huge and *seated on* a four-faced chariot called "Cherubin" [meaning child angel attendant on the Abrahamic God]. The Cherubin has eight *figures for* each [one] of the four corners, [meaning in Leo] lion forms and [meaning in Taurus] calf forms and [meaning in Aquarius] human forms and [meaning in Scorpio] eagle forms. *These* forms *total* sixty-four forms - and [concerning the] seven archangels [of the hebdomad] that *are positioned to the face of* it; he is the eighth [one above them] and has *power. In total they* amount to seventy-two [and are encoded in the human Tree of Life and the beat of the human heart].

THE MAJOR ARCANA (TAROT) REVEALED

It is said that the Major Arcana represents the stages of life, spiritual ascension, and evolution. It would appear that Antoine Court de Gebelin was right when he indicated that the tarot has its origins in ancient Egypt, and has mystic, divine and kaballistic significance. Ettiella, founder and propagator of divinatory tarot, continued this idea by claiming the tarot to also have an ancient Egyptian origin and to be an account of the world's creation. One need not be reminded, of course, that Nag Hammadi is a place in Egypt, and these are Egyptian texts.

It appears that what we are dealing with here, in this codex, is the Major Arcana (Great Secret); a book long searched for and now found. This codex appears to be the written evidence of the "hidden knowledge" spoken of and offered by Jesus to Judas Iscariot, Mary Magdalene, and all humanity when he spoke about "revealing" to them "great secrets". Indeed, the revealing science of God is one of the main themes of the library overall.

What we have today in the Major Arcana suit of the tarot is but a pale shadow of the erroneously named book On the Origin of the World. To give it its true title, the Book of Great Secrets, is a somewhat distressed, fragmented record of those ways, philosophies and expertise taught by adepts in that great time. This is why study of these codices is crucial outside of scholarly and religious framings.

> *In addition*, from *the motion of this* chariot, the [sacred] seventy-two gods *formed to* rule over the seventy-two *communication codes* of the peoples (one of which being the beat of their hearts). And by that throne [astrological term for a planet which sits on its throne when in a sign of which it is a ruler] he *generated* other, serpent-like [elemental] *powers*, called "Seraphin", which *serve* him *continuously*.

Seventy-two is also the number of years the earth takes to travel one degree around the zodiac. It is curious to note that according to the Neoplatonists and Neopythagoreans (1st century BC–2nd century AD), the planets and constellations communicated to the earth in codes. *The heavens speak to the earth. "The great thinkers* [of late antiquity, the Neoplatonists and the Neopythagoreans] *represent a body of knowledge we haven't even touched on. We are stuck in a modern paradigm. The ancients believed the planets communicated to the earth...They had access to the Library of Alexandria for 600-years."* – (Late) David Flynn, *The Earth-Mars Connection: Cydonia in Ancient Science and Mythology* (lecture), 2005.

Further to these communication codes, the chakras have been linked to the seven bodies of the solar system that are visible to the naked eye. Different schools of thought cannot agree on a definitive system or labelling. Across the NHC, where this occurs, the root would appear to be the planet Mars. The crown is the sun. Some models place the sun at the solar plexus, but this may be an error. For the sun to be so placed would strongly suggest a sun-centric rather than an earth-centric model of the solar system and the heavens. Hence, the Gichtel system largely adopted by the Theosophical Society may be incorrect because we should remember that in the Nag Hammadi library, the earth is flat and at the centre of the universe. Furthermore, the greatest thing on the earth is the human being.

ANALYSIS OF 21 OF THE MAJOR ARCANA -
Interpretation of this Card

The four corners are the four houses or star signs that appear fixed to the naked eye. The eagle is an ancient representation of the sign of Scorpio. Each house emerges from a cloud of celestial origin. Often overlooked in this card is the number 21 in Chaldean numerology, which means Crown of the Universe, achieved after many struggles and trials and which none shall take away, here worn by the (sometimes called) Divine Sacred Feminine at the centre of the world, now revealed as Sophia! She is replete with a garment draped across her figure in the form of a single helix representing her single female instructing principal in the form of the kundalini energy she brings. It also states in this codex that, 'the two bulls in Egypt hold a secret, the sun, and the moon, being [evidence and] a witness to Sabaoth: explicitly, that over them, Sophia took control of the universe; from the moment she completed [both] sun and moon, she set a seal upon her heavens, forever.'

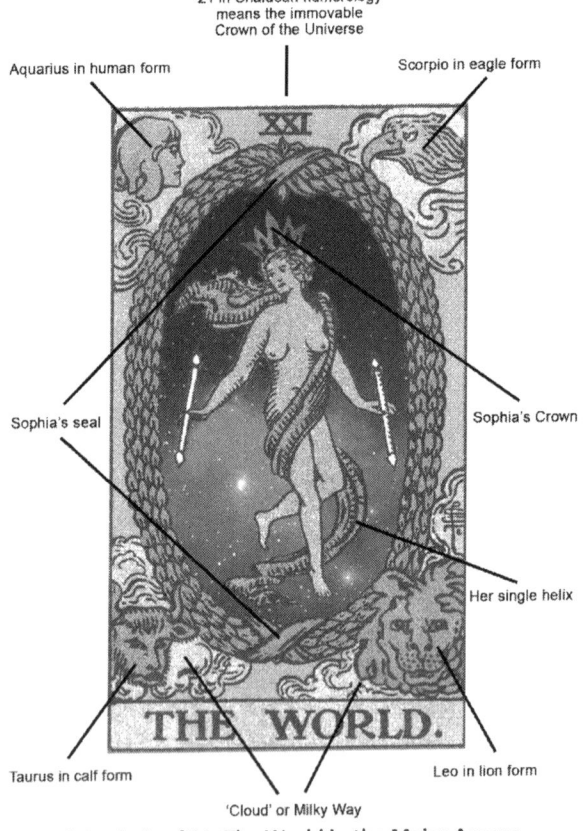

(Fig. 11) Analysis of 21, The World in the Major Arcana.

SOPHIA COMPLETES THE SUN AND THE MOON

Where the texts say that the trinity of the earth, moon and sun possess a mystery (secret), that is, the 'two bulls; maybe the answer (or a substantial part of it) can be found in how the eclipse of sun and moon can sometimes resemble bullhorns. The greater significance of this event can be found in how the moon balances the energies of the earth and planets. Mainstream science, media and conventional wisdom (aided and abetted by state and corporate owned broadcasters) close their eyes to the extraordinary science that governs our celestial triad (See fig 6).

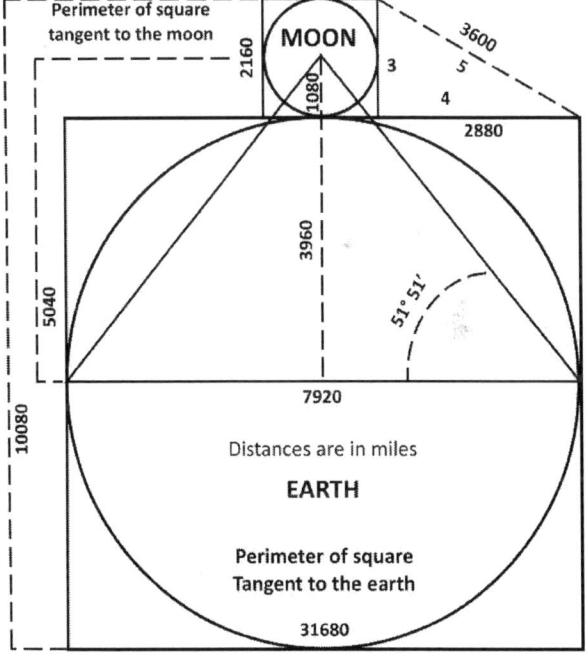

(Fig. 12) The moon squares the circle of the earth.

If one accepts the conventional models built by Eratosthenes, Copernicus, and 20th Century institutions such as NASA, then we only accept total eclipses as natural because we see them, but in truth, as 'total', they would be unknown anywhere else in the solar system.

THE TRINITY STANDARD OF 400

It is worth pausing for a moment to note some of the harmonies and mathematical correlations at work in the organising of the earth, moon and sun. Earth's meridian circumference in kilometres is 40,000. The earth turns 400 times faster than the moon. The moon's diameter is 400 times smaller than the sun. The sun is 400 times farther away from the earth than the moon. This is why the disc of the moon perfectly covers the sun during the rare cosmic phenomenon called a total eclipse. This type of lunar obscurity can only be seen from the surface of the earth. In order for the disc of the moon to appear the same size in the sky as the sun requires an amazing balance of energies between all the planets of the system. (*General source: Butler & Knight, 2005, Who Built the Moon, Watkins Publishing*).

It is interesting to note that unlike every other heavenly body, the earth, moon, and sun are without a name. They are known by what they are.

LUCIFER AS THE SUN, AND THE SUPPORT OF SOPHIA AND CHRISTOS

(20) *After that,* he *generated an endless, unlimited number of angels, forces and energies that were just like those of* the eighth heaven. And [joining him] *there was a firstborn who was named Israel* ("Is-ra-

el") [meaning the contraction of the name of the three gods, Isis-Ra-El] *and means* - "the [androgynous] man that sees God".

The next line makes little sense because it claims the presence of Jesus Christ next to the new sun. Although his coming is foretold in this codex, it is as the 'perfect human', not an elemental power. Also, 'the saviour' is a human being named Jesus, and Christ (redeemer, liberator). Therefore, what we are describing here is the spirit-powered Christos ray within the life-giving sun, in the same way Sophia's ray is also present. Both these rays are elemental and take on a double helix form.

> *The other being* [that was there] *was named* Jesus Christ who *was similar in appearance to the* saviour *up in the ogdoad and who is seated to his right on a venerated* throne.

In Pistis Sophia, (1896), Introduction, p. xxxii, G. R. S. Mead says of the work overall, *'...mistakes may have crept in. One of these copies was carried up the Nile and translated into the vernacular, Greek being but little understood so high up the river. The translator was evidently not a very accurate person, as may be seen from his casual insertion of scraps from other books moreover, his knowledge of the subject was so superficial that he had to leave [out] many terms in the original, and doubtless made guesses at others.'*

As students of these texts, we must remember that *they* and *we* are not infallible. We must make our own conclusions as to what each text really means and says to us personally. Further, the above quote is not an indictment of those who originally translated them. It is used here to illustrate that one must be cautious when interpreting them.

> And *to* his left sits [Eve] the virgin of the *divine female spirit*. And the seven virgins [spheres of the solar system] *rise* before her, [...] *each holding* thirty harps, and psalteries and trumpets, *circling* him.

*If you wish to see how the music of the spheres creates life and animates matter then research sacred resonances.

> And all the *legions* of *angelic beings give* him *illumination*, and they *exalt* him. Now where *Lucifer* [the celestial sun] sits is upon a throne of [bright shining] light within a great [celestial arch or belt] cloud that covers him, [he was alone there] in the cloud [with Pistis Sophia, revealing her 'forethought' and making known to him] all the things that *are* in the (Milky Way), so that the *re-creation* of those things *could now* be *replicated* [in the solar system], *so that* his *supremacy and control* might *continue through to* the *completion* of the *spheres* of chaos and their *powers* [meaning the full unified realisation of the Divine forethought and plan].

(21) *Then* Pistis Sophia set him *to one side*
from the darkness and *invited* him to [a
place at] her right [representing the astral
plane]. [Yaldabaoth] she *placed to* her left
[representing the lower nightmare level of
the etheric]. *From* that day, right has been
known as justice, and left *known as*
wickedness. *And as a result,* they *each*
received a *sphere* in the *assembly* of justice
and wickedness (heaven and hell
respectively), [where they *each*] stand [...*in
authority*] upon a creature [...*that resembles
a lion, one and*] all.

THE LION

The symbolic meaning of lions, as one might imagine,
primarily deals with strength. The fact that it is a
nocturnal creature means that the lion is a symbol of
authority and command over subconscious thought.
Night is an ancient symbol of the subconscious or
dream state.

MALEVOLENCE, INIQUITY AND ENVY EMERGE FROM YALDABAOTH

(22) *Once* the *chief father* of chaos
witnessed his son, Sabaoth, *together with*
the [radiant] *light in which he was bathed,*
and [in addition] *saw* that he was [the]
greatest of all the *archons* of chaos,
["Lucifer, leader of the angels"] he envied
him. And [filled with] *fury,* he [decided to]
bring about *Death and error [in the
hebdomad] *for the sake* of his death (and
error). And Death and error *became*

established [as the pattern] over the sixth heaven, *because* Sabaoth had been *quickly moved upwards* from there [rendering him untouchable]. And *so*, the *sum total* of the six *Great Archons* of chaos was achieved [for the loss of the one]. Then Death and error, *favouring neither male nor female, entwined* with his (own) nature and *he grew from out of himself offshoots of* seven *similar children* [as his archon instruments].

*See Glossary.

What follows is Yaldabaoth's counter to Sophia's works. She, being the creator come transformer, and he, the destroyer/saboteur. It is important to remember that the archons have sabotaged the human body and soul in order to destroy (you) the sacred, eternal spirit that incarnates therein. The vices listed below are the source of all our negative traits such as greed, hunger, sexual deviancy, addiction, envy, and hatred (*et al*). If you doubt any of these things, then consider this; the jails are full of people (lost spirits) who cannot control these negative traits that the archons have embedded in two of the three component parts of the tripartite human being from the start. The lesson offered is this: take control of that which errs within you, and you will find salvation and happiness immersed in the eternal joy and power of the Spirit. Hence, the virtues installed by Sophia will run counter to the negative traits, influences and power of the demiurge and will remain in place despite his best efforts and those of his created retinue. It is the freewill of the sovereign human being that reigns supreme and determines the outcome of one's true spiritual nature. This shall become clearer to you as we progress along the timeline.

VICES AND VIRTUES OF THE SOUL

*The seven masculine **vices** of the soul or psyche:*
Jealousy, *Madness, Crying, Depression, Pain, Sorrow,* Bitter *Tears.*

*The seven feminine **vices** of the soul or psyche:*
Madness, Pain, Lust, *Depression,* Curse, Bitterness, [and] Quarrelsomeness.

Each one [then] *generated and spawned* seven, *totalling* forty-nine *hermaphrodite* demons [in all]. Their names and their [negative] effects [on the human soul] you will find [recorded] in the *Book of Solomon.*

The virtues of the soul or psyche:
(23) And in the *company* of these, Zoe, who was [joined] with Sabaoth, [as a counter] *generated* seven *virtuous* androgynous *powers.*

The male ones are *known as*: the *Kind,* the Blessed, the Joyful, the True, the *Generous,* the *Cherished,* the Trustworthy.

The female ones are *known as*: *Serenity, Happiness, Jubilation,* Blessedness, Truth, Love, Faith (Pistis).

And from these [powers come] many *virtuous* and *innocent spirits. [You may find] their influence and effects [on the human being] in the *Configurations of the Fate of Heaven That Is Beneath the Twelve* [astrological houses].

*These are (we) the *little innocent spirits* generated to fight the archons, so identified further down in this text.

REVEALING OF THE TEMPLATE FOR THE HUMAN BEING
Destruction of the Archons, (continued)
And now we must take a leap back a little in the timeline in order to discover something else that appeared in the transformation of Sabaoth, namely, the revealing of the template for the human being. With it, she would trick the archons into making the bodily 'containers' for her light so that she might cleanse the planes of matter and ether of their wickedness and 'ruinous work'. And so, in this revealing, a grand deception was played upon the archons and their ruler by Sophia; an action which represented the beginning of her Divine Mission Plan, so defined through the creation of the three Adam and Eves. These are,

First, Lucifer and Zoe
Second, Satan (the reptile) and his equivalent Eve, (Pronoia).
Third, the Anthropos (androgynous human being) of the garden.

(24) And having *witnessed* the likeness [and forethought] of Pistis in the [cosmic]

waters, the prime parent *suffered* very much, *and even more so* when he *caught the whisper of* her voice, *because he recognised it as being the same voice* that, *deep in* the waters, had *beckoned* to him. And when he *realised* that she *was the one* who had [also created him and had sovereignty over him], he *groaned*. He was *humiliated through* his [error and] transgression. And when he *discovered the* truth, that an *eternal* man of light [a male power greater than him, the Christos aeon] had been *living previous to* him, he was greatly *worried because up until that time he declared* to all the gods and their *creations that he was* God *and that* 'no other one *existed* apart from *him*'. [And with some truth he said this for he was the only one they had perceived. Why?] *Because* he had *lived in fear of them* [ever] *discovering* that another had *existed prior to* him, and *therefore they* might *oppose* him [by becoming subordinate to that higher power at his expense]. But he, *entirely lacking* any understanding [by virtue of being a contrary thing of Death with no spirit in him, and pitiless], *laughed* at the *accusation* and *responded wildly by shouting*, "If anything has *existed prior to* me, let it *show itself*, so that *all might* see its light."

(25) And *at once, behold!* [as written] *light poured from* out of the [cosmic] eighth heaven above and *shot right the way* through *every heaven seen from* the earth. When *he* saw the *radiation and beauty of*

the light, he was *astonished and* was *put to shame by it* [such was its power and purity]. As that light appeared, *an amazing* human likeness [template] *became visible* within it. And *there was none other that* saw it *apart from* the *chief* parent and [his daughter] Pronoia, who was *aside* him. *Nonetheless, its* light [still] *became known* to *each of* the forces [energies and phenomena] of the *planets.* [And] they [became] *disturbed* by it.

(26) *After that,* when Pronoia saw that *representative* [vision of the Anthropos], she [could not help but] *become infatuated with* [and helically attracted to] him. But he *was repulsed by* her because she was *of* the darkness [of Yaldabaoth and he was of the light of Pistis Sophia]. But she desired to *take hold of* him *but failed.* [They were incompatible]. When she [found she] was unable to *contain* her love [for him], she *discharged* her *radiance* upon the earth. *From* that day, that (replicated) *representative form* has been *known as,* "Adam of Light," whose (physical) *image* is "the luminous man of *the bloodline,*" and the *material world* spread over him, [he who is] (i) holy Adaman, [and] whose image is "the *Divine feminine* Land of (ii) Adamantine."

This means her transforming power was spread the world over, creating the conditions to host all manner of organic life. The surface of the earth would now become poisonous to the archons, particularly in ET form.

(i) Holy in the NHC means female. See Glossary, Holy Spirit.
(ii) The *tine* suffix means "of or pertaining to", "of the nature of", "like".

> *From then on*, all the *archons* have
> honoured [meaning feared, respected, given
> service and continuity to] the blood
> [meaning life force] of the virgin [Pronoia
> by replicating, fashioning, and maintaining
> what was to follow in the world]. And the
> earth *became* purified *because* of the
> [etheric life] blood of the virgin. *More than
> that*, the water was purified *by way of* the
> *template* of Pistis Sophia and *materialised
> before* (Yaldabaoth) the *chief father* in the
> waters. *Rightly*, it has been said:
> [accomplished] "through the waters." The
> *Divine female* water vivifies [animates,
> activates] *everything* [and] *purifies it.

* Thereby making it fit to host. See Glossary, Oceanus.

EROS IS GENERATED AND DEFINED

The intelligent phenomenon that is called Eros suddenly appeared in the early creation of our biological world, helping to shape, form and reunify the dynamic relationship between the male and female halves that characterises the generating of organic life on earth. Eros also acts as a stabilising influence and catalyst amongst the soul-endowed emotional complexities of passionate spirits in human form, helping them to realise that, uniquely amongst the species of the earth, they are capable of unlimited love through, and in the face of, extreme adversity.

In the Orphic poetry (Orph. *Hymn.* 5; comp. Aristoph. *Av.* 695) he is described as *the first of the gods, who sprang from the world's egg.* (Paus. ix. c. 27.) [...he] *came into existence by himself.* Eros facilitated and functioned as the reunification of the male and female halves of the originally split androgyne through sexual union which is why all creatures leave their parents and seek union with another.

PRONOIA GIVES BIRTH TO EROS

(27) *From the* first blood [of the earth] Eros [a primordial androgynous god] appeared. His *masculine half* is Himireris [Desire], being fire from light [or soul from spirit]. His *feminine half* that is *within* him [is] a soul of blood [fiery-passionate nature and] is [made] from the *phenomena* of [the aforementioned] Pronoia. He is *exquisitely beautiful and has an allure over every* creature of chaos [so that] when all the *powers* and their angels *saw* Eros, they became [smitten, infatuated and under his spell] ...

Eros now becomes the embodiment of her uncontained love for the representative form she saw, transferred onto (and realised through) the creation of life on earth.

...She materialised in them all like a flame that sets everything alight without diminishing itself. And in this way, [the flame of] Eros *was spread to* all the *generated* beings of chaos, *without becoming weakened* [or reduced]. *In the same way that he was centred at* the midpoint of [both] light and *dark, he also* appeared at the midpoint of *both* angels and mankind. [And hereafter,] the sexual *bringing together by* Eros was *completed* (Major Arcana: The Lovers).

6 in Chaldean numerology meaning sensuality and maternity

Sophia oversees her creation of an earthly, organic bio-realm

Sabaoth transformed into the sun

Tree of Knowledge

(Firey soul) Tree of Life

Eros 'appears at the midpoint' bringing the gender halves together

(Fig. 13) Eros appears at the midpoint.

So, *on* the earth the *primary desire* blossomed. [This is the cycle of earthly life]. *The woman fulfils the earth. Union fulfils the woman. New life comes forth from that union. The earthly life ends in death.*

(28) *Then*, Eros the grapevine, *grew and developed from* that blood (a fiery-passionate nature), which had been shed [all] over the earth (like a connecting vine). *And it is for this reason, all that* drink of it *experience within themselves* the desire of sexual *consummation.* The grapevine *was followed by the* fig tree and [then came] a *pomegranate tree [and then rose and blossomed up all the trees and species] from the earth, [each] *containing* the seed of the *archons* and their angels.

*Pomegranate means 'apple' 'seeded' and is of Indo-Persian origin and represents fertility and reproduction. The NHC symbolism and meaning of the fig tree will become clearer in the soon-to-follow Garden of Eden scenes.

THE SCALES OF JUSTICE
(Judgement card 20, Major Arcana).
The following passage is very difficult to translate so, as before, with liberty of your interpretation, the author offers the following understanding.

(29) *Then* (i) Justice (also known as the Egyptian female aeon, Maat) *created a beautiful Paradise* (a heavenly state of being) *where none existed before, namely, in the* (ii) *Land of Wantonness, in the East, in the heart of the stones that was outside the orbits of the moon and sun. And that which is sought-after, longed for and craved*

can be found there at the centre of the beautiful, enticing trees. And the spirit tree of eternal life emerged and became visible by God's power, in a place that is to the north/top of the crown chakra of Paradise, so that it could make (iii) *everlasting the souls of the pure spirits,* [including the yet-to-be-created human beings] *who shall arise from their modelled bodies when this age shall reach its end.* (Fig. 15).

(i) So, Paradise is not always a geographical or physical place. It is an astral paradise and state of mind, balance and measure for the spirit-endowed ones who have led a physical life. It was created to draw to it these spirits for judgement, correction and meter, either by way of law, desire, or both, to remedy, instruct and make known to them the Divine pattern, formulation and plan, and their role in it. It can also represent the pattern of reincarnation.

(Fig. 14) The calling of the dead to Judgement.

The diverse trees are a metaphor for the patterns of all things. This Paradise is the gateway or ascension to spiritual truth and realisation on the part of the individual, away from the lower-order poverty of the demiurge's creation.

(ii) Imagine, if you will, an etheric place called Wantonness, so named because it is characterised, in extravagant form, by the traits of depravity, debauchery, immorality and shamelessness that sits on the low border of Tartarus and the higher limit of the astral plane as a domain of wretchedness. And where this problem looms, Sophia's instrument of correction, Justice, proudly builds her dwelling place.

In the translation of this codex by Willis Barnstone and Marvin Meyer, (2003), they interpret *'the land of Wantonness'* as *'in the luxuriant earth'*. How can one have faith in these orthodox translations when, in parts, they can be so different? So, is the interior of the earth then luxuriant?

Wantonness as a Physical Place

Also, the re-emergence of the flat (disk) earth belief system finds support here because, according to it, the once tropical paradise of Antarctica would be *'outside the orbits of moon and sun.'* The Age of the Lion was 12,500 BC, speculated as the time of Atlantis, and when the last great destruction and shift in the earth's axis took place. A growing number of professional thinkers, aided by hard, physical evidence, now surmise a pole shift occurred causing that tropical paradise to freeze over to become Antarctica. Carlos Muñoz Ferrada said that when Hercolubus returns, Brazil will become the new North Pole. These tangents are worthy considerations for readers when attempting to put into context the claims of cosmic catastrophe made within the library.

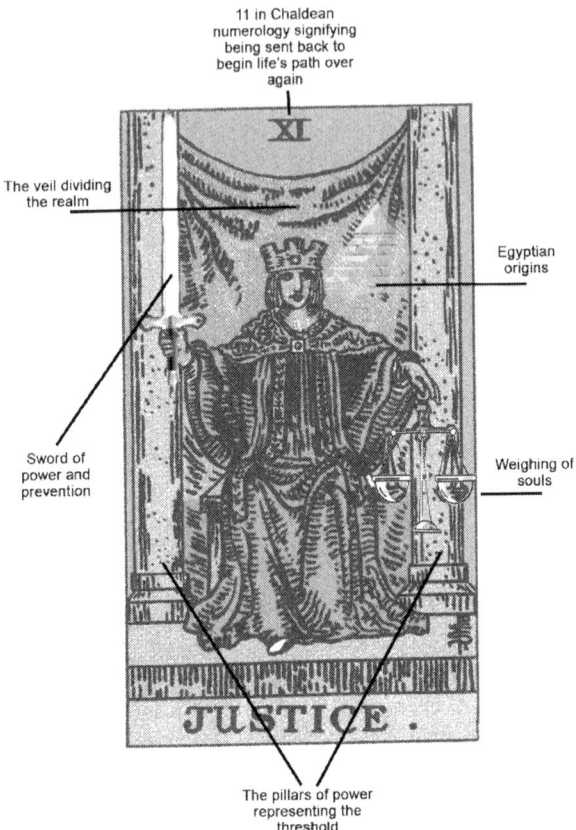

11 in Chaldean numerology signifying being sent back to begin life's path over again

The veil dividing the realm

Egyptian origins

Sword of power and prevention

Weighing of souls

The pillars of power representing the threshold

(Fig. 15) How Maat is delineated in the tarot.

(iii) Justice is personified by the female goddess, Maat, now properly identified on 11 of the Major Arcana suit. She is also often depicted in the Solar Barge of Ra together with her male aeon, Thoth. After helping maintain order in the cosmos, at the *end of the age* she takes on the role of allowing (through) into the spirit realm proper, those whose spiritual nature has remained sufficiently untarnished by archon influence;

put simply - those who are good. And where those who have failed now seek refuge from their deeds, they are met by the raised sword in her hand, barring any further progress on their part, forcing them back. In Chaldean numerology, 11 means those who fall under its influence are destined to begin life's path over and over. It is ominous to occultists and means hidden danger and strange fatality. The lower realms confine those who have engaged in the works (knowingly or not) of the demiurge, he who is sometimes referred to in the Coptic as Isfet.

The Libran scales are the instrument by which all souls are weighed in respect of righteousness and unrighteousness against Justice Maat. (Fig.16) The scale on the left shows her wearing the peacock feather. Also present is Anubis, the jackal-headed god, whose charge it was to take care of the dead. His hand steadies the scale. On the right is Horus, the falcon-headed god, weighing the heart of the figure on the right who kneels with hand over heart. He, too, steadies the scale. If Maat does not move, then they are allowed to pass through and take their place in the afterlife. Her peacock feather, for the reason of its lightness, symbolises the delicate nature of that balance where the weight of a feather can determine the outcome. Bad deeds and actions add weight to the heart which they believe formed from a drop of the mother's blood upon conception. It was considered the seat of the spirit, soul, and personality.

(Fig. 16) Section of the Judgement of the Dead. *Spell 125.* Liverpool World Museum.

Justice is an essential stage to fully developing into a human, but only up to the apprentice or beginner level - something also accredited to Jesus' mission in the texts. The added purpose of her scale is to prevent the universe returning to 'chaos'. She makes her presence, power and influence known when creation or the universe is in danger of becoming imbalanced through the actions of 'injustice', 'chaos' and 'violence'. Hence, she creates a paradise, a refuge, and a point of attainment in difference to the lower order chaos; the point in the crown chakra of the human being where her name literally means world order or world harmony.

THE TREE OF LIFE

Etched into the stone above the entrance to the Oracle at Delphi is the following quote, *'Man, know thyself and ye shall know the universe and its Gods'* [powers]. Adepts maintain that we each have a fully illumined tree of life within us. The seasonal, illuminated Christmas tree we enjoy each year, when replete with wrapped gifts and its faux star atop it, is but a shabby copy of the true Spirit and the gifts of love that light up the Tree of Life contained within you. Like so much in our world, it would appear the original message of the tree has been lost through archon manipulation and turned into something akin to human greed, competition, and enslavement rather than a representation of ascension and spiritual advancement. All that notwithstanding, the traditional celebration of Christmas is not something that is necessarily evil, rather, done in error of the model.

Further below, this codex makes it clear, *'you are the tree of knowledge'.

The rest of paragraph 29 is very difficult to interpret so it is here below reproduced in plainer English with liberty of interpretation.

> *To the top of the aforementioned Paradise is the tree of knowledge (gnosis), set there to awaken souls from the deep inertia of the demons so that they can be free to come (and find their way) to the (sacred) tree of knowledge and consume the fruit of its (wonderful) knowing, and become enlightened enough to enable them to push away the archons and their angel retinue. The tree is able to do this because it contains the Power of God. Its magnificence shines similar to* [that of] *the moon when full. And its branches* [too] *are resplendent. It has leaves that resemble those of the fig tree. And as for its fruit, its taste and*

appearance are like *that of an* appetizing date. *Its effects are found recorded in the Sacred Book, which makes it clear that where this tree grows in Paradise, *it is you who are the tree of knowledge. And from that same tree the first man consumed its fruit, and his mind was opened. It also says,* 'he loved his female *equivalent* and *despised* the other, alien *images* and *reviled* them.' *Now next to it grows the sacred tree of life whose* colour *is similar to* the sun [and whose] branches are *resplendent. It has* leaves *similar to* those *found on* the cypress [tree]. *It brings forth* fruit *that resembles* a *cluster* of (white) grapes. It *reaches all the way up to* heaven.

(Fig. 17) An example of a Sumerian Tree of Life, British Museum, London

(30) *Then* the olive tree *sprang* up *so as to cleanse the high servants [of God] by the light of Adam of the Luminaries – first Adam, Lucifer, the sun.*

THE CREATING PRINCIPAL BREATH

Next, we are given an order of generated things in which each one appears as the finished article.

(31) The first soul [principal breath] loved Eros. *The rose appeared out of the thorn bush to be a source of joy. Then came the sweet, scented flowers. Then came every plant containing the seed of the archons and their children. Then the archons created out of the shadow-waters all species of beast, and the reptiles and birds - different kinds - containing the seed of the archons and their angels* [the vivification process].

(32) *Then the earth was left in darkness by Eros's departure and *Lower Sophia was engaged and guided by Pistis power to fashion the great luminous bodies and stars of the sky to shine upon the face of the earth, and act as both clock and calendar for the subdivision and measure of time. Thus, all the sky was bejewelled.*

*Here we see the lower Sophia (Yaldabaoth is sometimes credited for this) acting as a proxy for the creation of the cosmos.

'ADAM OF LIGHT' IS LUCIFER THE SUN

(33) Now *as for* when Adam of Light *tried* to *access* his light *in the* eighth heaven *he could not*, because the *archon elements* that had *mixed* with his light [now rendered him adulterated].

In the Judas codex, Jesus reiterates this point by making it clear that *Adam of the Luminaries* was unable to enter the sacred realm of the spirit. Jesus describes him as Adamas who was the first that came before all in place and time as a bright shining cloud that no *messenger of the Spirit* had ever seen, even *amid* all those that were known as 'God.'

Judas asked him about the destiny of (this 1st) Adam and the human race. Jesus says, "Why *do* you *doubt* that Adam, *his span of life, together* with *his creation, have* lived *a prolonged existence in the company of* his ruler, *Saklas* (Yaldabaoth). *Has he not been given his monarchy there?'* (Bestowed as king of the sky).

Our sun is more than an 'unexceptional' star, as orthodox science tries to maintain. Instead, it is a living thing, endowed with super complex energies of ether, shadow and matter. The light it produces is the giver of life, the vivifier. Organic life cannot exist without it, save for that which is abysmal. For instance, what flower can grow by the light of a fire or flame? In the electric universe theory, the dynamo sun is a transceiver and will only end when all matter dies.

It is worth remembering that the Judas codex was not found amongst the NHC yet shares with it many concordances such as what follows in the next part.

Thus, he *fashioned* for himself *an immense, everlasting domain.* [An illumined solar system]. And within *it* he *made* six *everlasting worlds* and their adornments. [They equal] six in number [and he is the seventh]. *They* were seven times *superior to the unadorned model that had existed prior. Their* arrangement *is* written in the *Seventh Universe of the Prophet Hieralias* [meaning the hebdomad].

SOPHIA'S GRAND DECEPTION

(34) This passage describes how, even before Adam of Light had settled in his place in the universe, the archons turned on their prime parent, mocking him for his deception and lies at proclaiming himself as *"God"*, and that *"no other exists prior"* to him. The archons put him to task saying, *"But wait. Isn't this the god who has destroyed all our work?"* They were referring to 1st Adam. *"Yes,"* he replied, and then added, *"If you want him stopped then we should create for ourselves a human* (3rd Adam) *from the substance of the earth that is consistent with the pattern of our body, and consistent with the pattern of this being we saw in the revealing matrix of Sophia. It will be our slave; so that when he* [the sun] sees *that part of himself* [in the human being], he [like us] might [also] become *infatuated and captivated by* it.

They reason that if he sees a key part of himself in the human being then he will nurture it and help it to flourish, while, for their part, the archons will enslave those incarnated down into these bodies from the spirit forever.

And so all this fell in line with the [divine] forethought of Pistis, *so that mankind* should appear *on the earth this way* and *signal the beginning of the end of* [the archons] *by way of them* [making that spirit-imprisoning] modelled form.

The passage concludes –

And [hence] *that* modelled form became a *prison for* the *spirit.*

(35) [Thus] the *archons acquired* the knowledge (gnosis) necessary to create [a] man [3rd Adam]. Sophia Zoe - she *who sits* with Sabaoth [Lucifer] - had [already] anticipated *their actions* [by way of the gift of (mother) Sophia's forethought].

We are told her reaction to this was to 'laugh' at their intention. Laugh and laughed is a term used a lot in the NHC; fifteen times in the Judas codex.

They are blind: *oblivious to* their own [best] interests, they *unwittingly* created [3rd Adam]! *They acted in total ignorance of* what they *were* about to do. *Using forethought,* she anticipated *their actions* and *completed* her own man first. [He - 2nd Adam, Satan] was [created to] instruct *the* [human being] how to *revile* them and, *by doing so, escape their clutches.*

THE CREATION OF THE INSTRUCTOR, 2ND ADAM - MAN OF SOULS

(36) *Here is how the creation of the instructor happened. Under the direction of Sophia, a bead of spirit light from her light was dropped onto the water whereupon it turned into an androgynous human being. Next, she transformed it into a female body. Then she used it again to change into the mother* [Sophia - the pattern of] the mother [is also in the daughter], *which had appeared.* And he *completed* it in twelve months (one cycle of his orbit). *Thus, was created a human figure, neither male or female, whom the Greeks call his father, Hermes, and his mother Aphrodite (or Hermaphrodites), and* the Hebrews call Eve (Zoe, *spreader of life*) [wife of Lucifer], [she is] namely, the female ['instructing' principal] of life [the serpent in the garden]. [And] her *child* is the *being* that is lord [Adam of Souls]. Afterwards, the *archons* called it [Satan] "Beast", so *as to* lead *away* their *fashioned mortals* [because they made him into a god]. [Let it likewise be clear,] the *clarification* of the *one that is* "beast" is

[also] "the *teacher*". For [Satan] was *created* to be the wisest [meaning he was possessed of 'wisdom' and was god] of all [the earthly] beings.

In orthodox teachings and scripture, Lucifer, bringer of light, was an archangel, the brightest and most beautiful and beloved of the angels of Yaldabaoth, God of the Old Testament. When he created man in his image, he ordered all the other angels to worship his image in this man. Lucifer refused saying they are people made merely of matter whereas we are made from the fire of the soul, and hence he was banished. He grew in his arrogance and contention and began to challenge God. Because of this he lost his heavenly place and was cast down to Earth until the end of time. In the Old Testament he is depicted as an opposer or an accuser. But if we take Satan as the inspiration behind the serpent in the Garden of Eden then there is an argument for saying that Satan is trying to give humanity wisdom and knowledge so that he can raise the human being to the level of gods. But God steps in and puts a stop to his plans and this becomes the battle between the two.

In the Book of Job, Satan is on the council of God and there is a meeting. God says, *look at Job, a very faithful and obedient servant, to which Satan says, what do you expect if you give him everything? Take from him everything and see what happens.* Through these exchanges, Satan is established in scripture as the first adversary to God. Armed with our new understanding of the NHC, the Book of Job may now become a little clearer to you with respect to the status of its main characters and their dynamic.

ENOCH, CHAPTER 7-8 THE "WATCHERS"

In the *Book of Enoch*, the rebellion is led by a group of angels called the 200 Watchers, (alleged) helpers who interact with humans. They become enamoured of humans and create bodies, have children and marry. Their leader is Semjâzâ or Satanial who, like Lucifer, oversees the angels. He disagrees with God and wants to live alongside mankind in an attempt to share with us forbidden knowledge. In his book, *Oracle of the Illuminati*, 2004, William Henry is credited as being first to make the connection that the reptilian and grey aliens were known as archons by the early Gnostics.

The parasitic pattern of the archons under Lucifer's stewardship is perfectly delineated in the following passages from *The Book of Enoch*.

[Chapter 7]

1 And all the others together with them took unto themselves wives, and each chose for himself one, and they began to go in unto them and to defile themselves with them, and they taught them charms 2 and enchantments, and the cutting of roots, and made them acquainted with plants. And they 3 became pregnant, and they bare great giants, whose height was three thousand ells: Who consumed 4 all the acquisitions of men. And when men could no longer sustain them, the giants turned against 5 them and devoured mankind. And they began to sin against birds, and beasts, and reptiles, and 6 fish, and to devour one another's flesh, and drink

the blood. Then the earth laid accusation against the lawless ones.

[Chapter 8]

1 And Azazel taught men to make swords, and knives, and shields, and breastplates, and made known to them the metals of the earth and the art of working them, and bracelets, and ornaments, and the use of antimony, and the beautifying of the eyelids, and all kinds of costly stones, and all 2 colouring tinctures. And there arose much godlessness, and they committed fornication, and they 3 were led astray, and became corrupt in all their ways. Semjaza taught enchantments, and root-cuttings, 'Armaros the resolving of enchantments, Baraqijal (taught) astrology, Kokabel the constellations, Ezeqeel the knowledge of the clouds, Araqiel the signs of the earth, Shamsiel the signs of the sun, and Sariel the course of the moon. And as men perished, they cried, and their cry went up to heaven...

From-The Apocrypha and Pseudepigrapha of the Old Testament, R.H. Charles Oxford: The Clarendon Press.

The nearest human equivalent to an archon model is the sociopath. Many serial killers are of the same mind when it comes to the experiences of feelings and emotions. They will often say that when they kill, they do so in order to 'feel' - *'I wanted to feel something,'* - they say. True to the common thread of all world mythologies is the fact that gods (archons) cannot control their drives, especially when they take on human form or mate with human beings. That is why, at the end of this codex, they destroy everything and then destroy themselves. (Paragraph 68), They will be thrown *below 'into the abyss' where they will be annihilated because of all their works. It likens them to 'volcanoes' consuming one another through and by the hand of the demiurge, until nothing of them is left. He will then turn in on himself and destroys himself out of existence.*

In the Book of Enoch, we have the secrets of medicine, warfare and all the forbidden knowledge of the gods, bartered to the humans at an unsustainable price. Some scholars and commentators ask, is he really the epitome of evil or is this liberation? And others ask, are these things not the foundations for civilisation? The Watchers also appear in the mythological record as the Anunnaki reptiles and insectoids (ant people). Other similar references are seraphim, which means winged or fiery serpent, and raphin, meaning giant. And, throughout South America, Viracocha, the fiery winged or plumed serpent, sustains this contiguity with the image of the human coming out of the mouth of a serpent, signifying our origins in the helix form of the *charmed,* rising snake.

In the masculine dominant ideology of the Greeks, Prometheus [also Lucifer] - is often recognised as one of the creators of mankind. His name implies 'forethought'. He supported Zeus (the demiurge) during his war with the Titans. But because he stole fire [light] from Olympus and gifted it to the humans with which he had become so infatuated, he brought upon himself a tremendous vengeance at the hands of Zeus. Enraged, the aforementioned Zeus commanded Hephaestos to fashion a female called Pandora, the Greek Eve, and she was bestowed with sinister malignant powers. Her 'box' is a euphemism for her vagina, hence root chakra, which is credited with unleashing to the world all manner of plagues and evil. In *Prometheus Bound*, Aeschylus described him as the liberator or saviour. Shelley's poem of the same name takes the stance that he is an icon of those who dare to confront oppression for the sake of humankind. Wherever one looks, he is one figure in different languages and cultures!

THE ORDER OF THINGS

Creator of the Entirety creates Sophia.

Sophia creates Yaldabaoth.

Yaldabaoth births Sabaoth.

Sophia transforms Sabaoth into Lucifer.

Lucifer is Adam of Light (1st Adam).

Sophia gives to him her daughter, Zoe, in marriage.

Lucifer (Sabaoth) and Zoe give birth to Satan (2nd Adam, the reptilian).

Satan is Adam of Soul (soul-endowed).

Yaldabaoth creates (3rd) Adam (of Eden), the Anthropos (imperfect human being).

Sophia and Christos birth Jesus, (4th) Adam (the 'perfect human' being).

The Anthropos destroy Jesus, or 3rd Adam murders 4th Adam.

(37) Now, [as for] Eve, [she] is the *original* (i) virgin who, *out of wedlock, birthed* her first *child* [Adam of Light]. She *acted* as her own midwife. *That is why* she is *thought* to have *sung*:
I am part of my mother [Sophia]; *I am the mother.*
I am the wife; I am the virgin.

I am pregnant; I am the midwife.
I relieve the pains of labour.
My husband bore me; I am his mother.
He is my father and lord.
He is my force; His desires are declared
with purpose.
I am in the *course* of (ii) becoming; *still*, I
have *allowed* a man *to be master*.

(i) See Glossary, virgin. (ii) Weasel word.

OUR SPIRIT IS IMPRISONED BY THE BODY AND THE SOUL

(38) *And so, by* the will <...> [of Pistis] <...>
the *spirits* that were *set* to *go into* the
fashioned forms *created by* the *archons*
were *revealed* to Sabaoth [Lucifer] and his
Christ [part]. And *on the subject of* these,
the *divine* voice *declared*, "[Proliferate!]
Increase in number and *develop! Take
command of* all [the earth's] *living things*."
And it is *these ones* [meaning, the 'innocent
spirits' of which Jesus had spoken] who
[incarnated, that] were taken *prisoner, in
accordance with* their *fates, by Yaldabaoth.*
And, *as a species, found themselves locked
into* the *jails* of the [archon] *fashioned
bodies for* the *duration* of the age.

(39) *Yaldabaoth consulted with the Seven
Great Archons to make a plan. Accordingly,
he gave instruction to each of them to
spread their sperm throughout the
Anthropos world, meaning humankind came*

to be [modified and hence] *similar to them in the body, but with the* (i) *likeness resembling the heavenly Anthropos man which had originally materialised to Yaldabaoth and his daughter, Pronoia* [in the vision of Sophia]. *He fashioned and formed the human in single separate stages. He undertook the formation of the* (ii) *brain and generated the intelligence and also the system of nerves and likewise the soul. Later*, he appeared as *before* to him. He *grew into* a soul-endowed man. *They gave him the name* Adam, *specifically*, "father", *just like* the one *who appeared prior to* him [because Satan too was a god].

(i) *Likeness* here appears to mean distinct from the physical form, perhaps referring to the shape and pattern of the soul comprising its system of meridians, auras and chakras.

(ii) *Brain* can also be taken to mean intelligence. It is separate from consciousness and the spirit's abilities to empathise, imagine or feel, have compassion for and be capable of love. Concerning the mind, the soul, and the spirit, in the Mary codex Jesus says, *'where the mind is, there is the treasure.'* I [then] said to him, *'Do we see* a vision [a revelation] *by way of* the soul or *through* the spirit?' *and he* answered, *'No one sees with the soul or the spirit. Instead, it is through* the mind [that] *resides* between *the* two,' - meaning the *'mind is treasure'* because it contains the abilities of consciousness, critical thought and freewill, so endowed by Sophia.

(40) *After the archons completed* [the 3rd] *Adam, Yaldabaoth* [in great disappointment] *discarded him like a lifeless, motionless vessel, because he had formed similar to an abortion* [on the earth, meaning a poorly made thing], *and he was devoid of a spirit within. His aborted creation reminded him of what Pistis had said* [about the Christos personification appearing in these modelled forms] *and he became full of fear should* [Sophia's] *true man come into the Anthropos body he had fashioned and, hence, grow to become its master* [instead of him]. *So, he decided to leave it for forty days with no soul in it and he subsequently forsook it and departed. Then on the fortieth day came Sophia's daughter, Zoe the bringer of life, to give her breath* [meaning soul] *to the soulless Adam. And he became animated* [meaning alive] *upon the earth, yet unable to awaken.*

(41) [Now] *deeply disturbed at the sight of Adam* [in this state], *the Seven Great Archons decided to lay hold of him. Yaldabaoth approached and investigated his soul. "I want to know who you are, and from what place, or source, did you come here?" he asked. And the soul revealed* [its truth] *to him. "From the power of* [the] *Christos* [aeon, and Sophia's forethought], *I have come to destroy your work."* When *the archons found his truth,* they glorified him, *because* he *relieved them of the terror* and *stress* in which they *were immersed*

[perhaps meaning their own internal nightmare existence]. *And hereafter* that day *was known as the day of* "Rest", *because from* toil they [had] rested. *Upon seeing that* Adam *was able to* [at last] *stand aright,* they were *prepared,* and *moved* him *into* [the state of] Paradise. *Then* they *returned* to their *heavenly spheres.*

(42) *After which Zoe, the daughter of Sophia, also known as Eve, came for the instruction and awakening of the soulless Adam, that he should hence arise and create humans to be converted into* 'containers of light' [meaning spirit-endowed physical bodies].

The next part states that Eve saw her masculine equivalent lying flat or prostrate. It says she took pity on him and with her voice said, "Adam! *Wake up! Walk* upon the earth!" He responded to her voice immediately by rising. Instantly, her word became a proficient and consummate fact by virtue of him opening his eyes. Hence, he was able to see her and spoke thus, "You shall be called [the] 'Mother of the Living' *because* [it is] you who have *gifted* me life."

(43) Then the *archons became full of concern and worry when they learned that the modelled Anthropos Adam was animate and breathing and risen* [from the ground. And so] seven [archons] archangels *were dispatched down* to *Adam so they might see* what had *come about. They found* Eve

speaking with him. *To one and all they said,* "*How strange is this* luminous woman? *Look. See how similar she is to the image that materialised to us in* [Sophia's vision of] *light. Quickly,* [let us] *seize her* and *multiply* her *offspring* into her *to soil her so that* she *will never* ascend [back] into *the* light [from which she came]. *Instead,* [all] those [children to] whom she *will give birth shall come* [to be enslaved and] *under our control. We shall tell nothing of this to Adam* because he is of *a different type to* us. *Instead, we shall cause a profound amnesia to descend upon him.* And *we shall teach* him, in his *amnesia,* that she *was created* from his rib *so that* his wife *might become* [his] *subordinate,* and he may *have rule* over her."

EVE (ZOE, LIFE) AND THE TEMPLATE OF THE HUMAN

(44) But Eve, [she] being a [greater] *power, ridiculed* their *actions.* She *placed a* mist in their *vision* [in order to blur their perceptions and understanding] and *quietly and invisibly she* left her [sacred] *image* with Adam. She [the Divine life force and pattern] *went into* the [sacred] tree of knowledge and *stayed* there. *They chased after her, trying to break her pattern and code,* and she *ensured they knew* that she had *entered* the tree *to* become a tree. *And because of that,* the blind *beings took flight.*

THE RAPE OF THE HUMAN EVE

(45) *Then, after a time, they recovered* from their *bewilderment,* and *returned* to [their]

Adam; and seeing the [true Eve's replicated pattern of the tree of life in] this [fashioned] woman [figure who was still] with him, they *became deeply worried*, thinking [to themselves that it] was she. [They did not recognise her as being a different Eve, perhaps for the reason of the *mist* earlier placed in their eyes. They did not realise that this was the Eve they had split from the Adam androgyne. And so] *foolishly*, [with their hands] they *laid hold of* her [in order that they might] *spread* their seed [meaning offspring and descendants] upon her. They did so *fiercely and destructively, in all manner of ways, corrupting and violating first the divine pattern that had created her and* had [originally] spoken *through* them *when it asked*, "[Archons, you *believe yourselves to be* first but], *do you know* that *which has had life* before you?" [Their] *intention* [was] to *contaminate and pollute* [all] those who might [have a reason to] say at the *end* [of the age] that they *were* born [out] of the [one] true *Christos aeon* through [the Divine formulation and plan]. *And so, the archons erred, not having the nous within to realise they had achieved nothing other than the defiling of their own body:* it was *their pattern and image of the sacred tree of life* that they and their angels *corrupted* in every way.

*These two paragraphs (44 and 45) are essential in explaining paragraph 28 in *Testament of Norea* regarding her mother, Eve, where it says —

28. The *archons convened a meeting with* her, *deciding they would* [pretend to be something they were not and lead her into their ways instead of those of the Spirit].

The demiurge then says to her that her mother, Eve, had come to them, which was a lie. She scorns them for their nature and that, as rulers of the darkness, they are despised and doomed. She then adds,

"And *neither* did you *breed with* my mother; *rather,* it was your *feminine equivalent* you *bred with* [a female you yourselves created]. *You are in error because* I am not your *child*; rather it is from the *realm* above that I *have* come."

(46) *And so, consistent with the plan of Yaldabaoth, his first archon made her pregnant with one known as Abel. Then she birthed the children of the Seven Great Archons and their angel retinue. And all this was done in order that Eve, the original mother, could carry inside her, each seed, being diversified and varied, and hence, integral with the destiny and outcome of the universe, its arrangement and composition, as well as to the aforementioned Justice* [meaning spirits who do the work of the archons are sent back at the gate from entering the spirit world]. *And so, a pre-organised plan was implemented in respect of Eve for the entrapment of the* [human] *spirits of light,* [meaning] *they became slaves of the archons and the* [poor quality]

souls and bodies they fashioned.

THE THREE TYPES OF ADAM

(47) *The first day saw the creation of the first Adam, and he is called Adam of Spirit and Light, Lucifer. The sixth day saw the creation of the second Adam of soul, Satan, whom the Greeks also call Aphrodite. The eighth day saw the creation of the third Adam, and he is Adam of the earth, or the man made by God's law, meaning the one composed of the lower order creation which is called The Age of the Sun or, "The Day of the Sun"* (i) *(Sunday). And the descendants and children of the earthly Adam proliferated in great numbers. And this, in every respect, was accomplished so as to reveal within itself the total matrix of* (ii) *'scientific' data with regard to the soul-endowed Adam. But all these things, however well executed, were done in ignorance of how the spirit enters the body, animates it, and so becomes a reflection of God.*

(i) Now in respect of Sunday, the texts reveal here another connection to the Vedic and Hindu system of Indo-astrology in which Surya (also similar in name to Syria) fulfils the role played by Sabaoth as the 'chief' deity or 'ruler' of our planetary system. To this end he is often characterised upon a chariot drawn by seven horses representing the seven chakras of the soul and colours of the sacred rainbow spectrum when split into its principal rays. He is the presiding deity of the Age (or Day) of the Sun, "Sunday". (See Glossary, Sunday)

(ii) *'Scientific'* means that what is revealed through their continued experimentation, crossbreeding and alterations, is the entire blueprint for the human being.

(48) *Firstly, I shall* say that the *archons* were very *pleased to witness Adam* and the female, erring *unawares* like beasts. [But] when they *realised* that the *eternal* man [Christos] was not going to *go away and that, in fact, they* would *also* have to [exist in] fear [of] the *woman* that had *changed into* a tree, they were *troubled,* and *held,* "*Maybe* this [one] is the true man [of which we were warned] - this *one* who has brought a *confusion over* us and has *shown* us that she *whom we greatly defiled* is [after all just] like him - *by reason of which* we *will* be *defeated!"*

(49) *And so,* the seven *conspired to make* plans. *Hesitantly* [and with some trepidation] they *approached* Adam and Eve *saying, "You* shall *consume* [meaning absorb and take in] *the* fruit [meaning various enlightenments and gifts] of all the trees [that were] *made* for you in Paradise. *But concerning* the tree of knowledge, *you must exercise* control *over yourselves, and hence refrain* from *eating of* it. *Should you disobey and consume this fruit then* you shall die." *And* having *put their deep fear into* them, they *returned* to *their realm.*

(50) *Next into the garden* came the wisest

[meaning creature of wisdom and gnosis] who *went by the name* Beast [meaning reptile, meaning male, also known as Satan]. And *upon seeing* the *image* of their *life giver in the* Eve *woman* he *asked* her, "What did *god forbid* you *to do? Did he say that you were* not *to consume* the *fruit of* the tree of knowledge?" *Eve replied,* "*He forbid us not only to* eat from it [meaning take in, be filled and enlightened] but *also that we were* not *to* [even] touch it, *and that if we did then we would* die." [Satan] *the* [reptilian] *Beast* [created to lead them away from Yaldabaoth] *then* said to her, "*Have no fear. You will not suffer death. Instead, from its consumption shall your* intellect *grow. You will become clear of thought* [also gnosis] *and* grow to become *like gods, knowing* the difference between *good and evil men and that which takes hold of them. He said this* [to stop you consuming these fruits and becoming enlightened] *because he* [Almighty God] *is filled with envy* [towards you].

NAKEDNESS AND THE CONTROL OF THE 'ROOT' (CHAKRA)

(51) Eve *believed in what* [Satan] the instructor, *said.* She *fixed her gaze towards* the tree and *became aware, liking its great beauty* and *appeal*; [and so] she [decided to] *partake of* its fruit and [then] *shared it with Adam*; and *both became full.* Their [intelligence, mental power, and mind] *opened up. Because by eating the fruit of the sacred* tree, [it meant] the [burning]

light of knowledge *was able to pour out its radiance over* them. When they covered [the root chakra entry point of their loins] with 'shame' [it meant they were now enlightened and had an *ego], they [also] *recognized themselves as being* naked of [something else], 'knowledge'. When they *grew aware*, they *perceived their apparent nakedness* [this time meaning Eros] and [so] *grew to be in love* of *each other*. [But] *as soon as* they *realised* that *the creators* who had *fashioned* them *were* beasts [reptilian], they *despised* them: [for] they were [now] very *awake* [and conscious].

*When a child looks in a mirror and recognises the reflection as being its own, that is said to be the beginning of the ego. Awareness of oneself is a key stage to developing into a human being.

(52) *And so, the archons returned to Paradise having become aware that Adam and Eve had gone against their instructions. And they brought with them* 'earthquake' *and terror, curious* to see *for themselves* 'the effect of the **aid**' [Weasel word]. *In fear, Adam and Eve* 'hid *themselves beneath* the trees in Paradise' [of which they were now an enlightened part. And they 'hid', meaning they closed their root chakra entry point preventing the archons taking control of them]. *And the* rulers *knew not where they were* [meaning they could not control them]. "Adam, where are you?" *they asked.*

Then Adam showed himself, explaining,
"Here I am. I hid myself in fear [meaning he
closed his loin chakra] *for I was* 'ashamed'"
[meaning naked and open to their control].
And *in ignorance* they said, "Who
instructed you *concerning* the shame [of
your nakedness and exposure, hence]
causing you to cover yourself [with a fig
leaf from the sacred tree of knowledge,
thereby closing yourself to us? This you
could only have known by consuming] *its*
fruit!" Adam replied, "The *female* you *gifted*
me, she *gifted* to me instead and *so* I
consumed." And they turned to Eve [in
ignorance] *and asked, "Tell us what* you
have done." *And she replied, "I was*
encouraged to consume the fruit of the tree
by [Satan] the instructor."

THE ARCHONS DECLARE WAR ON SATAN AND THE WORLD

(53) *Next* the rulers *approached* the
instructor. *But because of his superior light,*
their perceptions of him became *hazy and*
indistinct and they were thus unable to do
anything to *stop* him. And *because of their*
weakness they *damned* him. *Then* they
approached the woman and *damned* her and
[all] her *children. Then* they *damned* Adam,
and [all] the *earth* because of him, *together*
with the crops; and *every part of their*
creation they *damned. The archons are*
without blessing [meaning gift or grace]
therefore no good *can come* from evil.

(54) From that *moment on,* the archons

where in no doubt of a greater power than themselves existing [in the universe]: they *acknowledged nothing else other than the fact that it was* only their *instructions that* had been *ignored. Tremendous envy then came* into the world solely *because* of the [fact and power of] the immortal man. *Once* the *archons became aware* that their Adam had *modulated and become endowed with* an 'alien state of knowledge' [meaning he had altered in a way unfamiliar to them, for he had progressed far beyond their plan], they *sought* to *re-examine* him. They *brought before him every conjugal animal* and wild *beast* of the earth and *fowl* of *the sky* [in order] to see what *names he might give to each of* them. *And so, he named each and every one of* their creatures.

(55) They *entered into a despairing state of mind* because Adam had [unexpectedly] recovered [and improved] from all *their experimentations.* They *communed* and *conspired together, making* plans *and saying, "Look* [at] Adam! He has *grown* to *become just like* us *in* that he *can now distinguish* between [that which is of] the *spirit* and [that which is of] the *shadow.* He *may possibly* now be deceived, as [he was when it came to] the Tree of Knowledge. [Therefore he] will *go to* the Tree of Life [containing the map and plan of the human soul] and *consume its fruits,* and *so be given immortality,* and *lordship,* and [hence] *look down on* us and *hold us* and all our glory *in contempt!* [That being so, he will] then

condemn us *and* our [entire] *created realm.* Come, let us *banish* him *out of* [his state of] Paradise, down to the [level of the] *material plane* from *whence* he *originated, in order* that he *will* not be [sufficiently] *intelligent* to [see and understand] anything *more* than we can." They *removed* Adam and Eve from [their states of] Paradise. *But it* was not enough [because the archons] were [still] *frightened* [by their potential]. They *entered* the Tree of Life *to place around* it [all manner of startling things that would cause great fear to rise in those who were tempted to follow therein. And these things were in the forms of] creatures *of flame known as* "Cheroubin" [meaning demons or negative angels of the demiurge], and they *were seen to place* a *burning* sword in their *heart*, fearfully *coiling without cessation*, so that no *human* being *could* enter [into] that place.

(56) [And] *because of their great envy, the archons sought ways in which to reduce the mortality of Adam and Eve, but found they were unable to do so* because of *an outcome that* had been *in place from the start.* For *they* each *were given* 1,000 years *in which to live in accordance with the plan of the* luminous bodies [of light]. *The seven archons failed, deciding instead to reduce their lives,* each *one of them, by* ten years *so that they now lived* 930 years [inverted to *70 years], *but* in pain, weakness, and *all manner of* evil distraction. *That is how* life has *become* from that day [and will be right

through] until the *completion* of the [3rd]
Age.

*Psalm {90:10} The days of our years [are] threescore
years and ten; and if by reason of strength [they be]
fourscore years, yet [is] their strength labour and
sorrow; for it is soon cut off, and we fly away.

(57) *So,* when *Sophia's* [daughter] Zoe,
witnessed the *archons* of the darkness
placing an affliction upon her [created]
equals, she [became extremely] *angry.*
[She] *burst from* the first heaven [carrying
with her] *tremendous* power [so that she
could] *chase the archons* out of their *realms*
and *hurl* them *downward* *into the *impure*
world [meaning the earth and material
plane, and lower astral], *where they could
live in* the form of evil spirits [and demons].

*This would appear to be a verification of the long-held
belief that so-called ETs and demons dwell within the
earth, and that they and the archons are one and the
same.

(Fig. 18) Zoe casts down the archons, and those who do their bidding.

THE PHOENIX AND TRANSMIGRATION OF THE SOUL

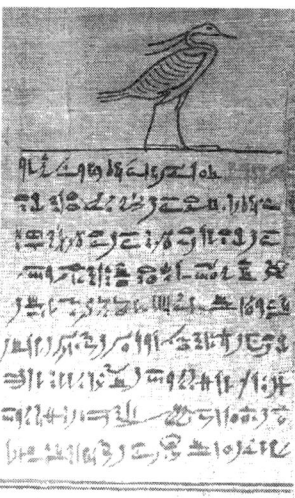

(Fig. 19) From the Book of the Dead, *spell 83* to transform the human into a phoenix. Liverpool World Museum.

(58) [Line missing], *in that aspect of the world controlled by the archons, the soul-endowed human being called "phoenix" may have* life for *one* thousand years in [a state of] Paradise. [Hence], it *dies of its own accord* [meaning in accordance with its own natural order] and *then resurrects* itself to life as *proof of* the *outcome that from the start had been in place* against *the archons*, [*namely that the archons are without a spirit and the spirit is the eternal part of the living human*]. *Because* [without doubt, what] they did to Adam, *including* his *offspring* [became the established pattern] *right through to* the *end* of the age [and was] *foul,* [and corrupt]. There are [known to be...] three [types of] men [meaning Adams], and *those who came after him right*

through to the *end* of *creation*. [These are],

The spirit-possessed of eternity.
The soul-possessed [of the astral].
The body-possessed [ones of the earth].

There are three phoenixes that live in Paradise.

The first one is eternal.
The second one lives for 1,000 years.
The third one is consumed (perhaps meaning made of matter).

It is also *recorded* in the *Sacred Book* that the latter is *destroyed*. [In the Judas codex, Jesus says all things dissolve into that from which they came, meaning matter dissolves into that which is of itself (meaning decay and alteration) and spirit, such as ourselves, return to from whence we came, the true Spirit Realm]. *In addition*, there are [a total of] three baptisms -

The first [one] is spiritual *in its nature* meaning of the spirit]
The second [one] is by *flame* [meaning of the soul]
The third [one] is [made] by water [meaning of the material plane].

In the same way the phoenix [man] appears [upon the earth] as a witness *to* the angels, so, [it is with] the water hydri (river) in Egypt.

This part of the passage also references a physical baptism by submergence in water to symbolised becoming a 'true man'.

The two bulls [perhaps symbolising the sun and moon, night and day, light and dark] in Egypt *hide a secret*. The sun *of the day* and the moon *of the night* witness [the truth of] Sabaoth [and his transformation into our sun]: namely, that over them [and by reason of this] Sophia *obtained* the universe; from the *time in which* she *completed* [both the formation and positioning of] the sun and the moon, she *placed* a seal *around* her heaven, *to last for* eternity [and depicted in 21 of the Major Arcana of the tarot] (See fig. 11).

(58) And the worm [meaning kundalini serpent stream] that *was* born *from* the phoenix is [also] a human being. It is *recorded in* (Ps 91:13 LXX) *regarding* it, "the *righteous, virtuous* man will *flourish* like a phoenix" [meaning his ascension to the Spirit World is assured without incident].

The Old Testament version of this is different and reads, *'Thou shalt tread upon the lion* [Yaldabaoth] *and adder* [his serpent daughter Pronoia]*: the young lion* [Sabaoth-Lucifer] *and the **dragon** [meaning the reptile beast, Satan]* *shalt thou trample under feet*].

And the first *incarnation of the* phoenix *is as a mortal,* and dies, [and then] *lives once more as* [clear] *proof of what shall happen when the end of the world comes* [meaning, as Jesus said, everything will dissolve into that from which it came]. *Because of its similarity to* Paradise, it was *uniquely and exclusively* in Egypt that these great *things were shown.*

*At the time of the building of the great monuments, such as the Sphinx, you may be surprised to learn that Egypt, North Africa, and the Middle East, were once tropical paradises, and not the parched, near baron landscapes we see today. For context and widening the scope of your understanding of the NHC, you might want to spend some time researching world catastrophe in prehistory.

EXPLANATION OF THE ARCHONS

(60) *Now I shall* return to the *subject of the archons in order to put before you* some *kind of* explanation *regarding* them. *Consider this*, *at the time* the Seven [Great] *Archons* were *ejected* from [out of] their heavens [down] *to* [Mount Hermon on] the earth [plane], they [set about] *creating* for themselves *an abundance of* angels, [and] demon-*like* [entities], to [be under their control]. And *those* [Enochian "Watchers"] *that were demonic, taught humans* [many distractions and] *ways to* 'error' [meaning wrongdoing] and [to create spells, chants,

prayers and incantations] and potions [meaning substances that can enhance for a time but ultimately destroy the psyche, the body, the intelligence, the mind and the spirit]. And worship of idols [so as to divert people away from the true pleroma] and *letting* of blood [upon the earth, indicating wars] and altars and [the building of] temples [of worship to them] and [the making of blood] sacrifices and libations [meaning brews] *poured out as offerings* to *all the false* spirits of the earth, *who coexist with those who are in error with them so that they might share their* fate. *They sprang* into *being because of* the *unity that thrives amid* the *powers* of injustice and justice.

(61) And *so, from the time,* the world [had originated,] *developed and taken form*, it *was consistently in a state of error and distraction. Why? Because* all [the] men [of the] earth [were given over to the] *worship [of these] spirits [and demons] from *beginning to end* - both the *angelic beings* of *virtue and justice* and the men [who flourish on] *vice and iniquity. And so, as a result* the [whole] world *came* to [be characterised by] *diversion* [and disturbance and] *blindness*, and [all] *under* a [heavy] *trance* [and amnesia]. *And so it was that* they all erred, until the *arrival* of the "true, [perfect] *human* [being]" [the personification of the Christos aeon].

*Throughout these codices, ceremony and worship of any kind is, for the most part, considered distraction and error – though there are parts of the library that might contradict this statement, accurately translated sections notwithstanding, of course. They say beware of intercessors who come between you and that which created you. Consider this. What parent demands that their children bow down and worship them? What God tells his most faithful servant to take his only begotten, and most beloved son, up a mountain to sacrifice him by plunging a dagger into his heart, as with the testing of Abraham's loyalty? All these things are the product of insanity and evil. They are not the product of love or anything you would want in you.

(62) Let *what is written up to now be enough in* so far as *this* matter goes *because* we now *must move onto the* [subject of the] *contemplation* of our world *to complete, with accuracy, the explanation* of its *formation* and *organisation. So,* it will [then] become *clear* [to you] how *faith and trust* in the [Spirit] *world that is not visible to you, but was evident from start to end,* was *revealed.*

(63) *And so,* I come to the *most important thing about* the immortal man: I shall *tell you about* all the beings that *have their place in* him, *and by doing so I will shine a light on* how they *came* to be here.

THE RAISON D'ETRE OF LIFE
(64) When *an abundance* of *people had been born who were descended from* the

[3rd] Adam, [the human who] *was formed from* matter [by the archons], and [hence] the *earth* became full [of his offspring], the *archons* were [the] *controllers of* it - *meaning*, they *held* it by *restraint and* ignorance. *Here is the reason. Because the Creator of the Entirety has full knowledge of the* deficiency of truth [that] *occurred* amongst *these everlasting worlds* and their universe, he *decided* to bring *them to an end,* the *archons* of ['perdition'] *ruin and eternal punishment,* [by] *using* the *humans* they [themselves] had *fashioned and formed*, [and so] he *incarnated* them *downward* into the [archon ruled] world of *ruin and eternal punishment, meaning* [you], the *gifted and graced* little innocent spirits. [You] are not *without* knowledge *and understanding* [meaning you are capable of comprehending that which is beyond the archons]. *Because* all knowledge *can be found* in one 'angel' who *was generated* before them; he [the Christos] is [certainly] not without power [and influence] *when in the company of* the [Entire] Creator. And [Word missing: Speculation: *he*] *bestowed* [to] them knowledge [and understanding]. *Where* they *occur* in the world of *ruin and eternal punishment,* *at once* and *above all* they *make known* [by example] the pattern [and reality] of *immortality,* [thus standing] as a *denunciation* of the *archons* and their *powers. And so,* when [you] the [graced and gifted immortal spirit] beings *materialised* in [the] forms [of shadow and matter]

modelled by [the] *archons* [of that darkness], they were envied [for their immortal spirit light]. And *because of their colossal* envy, the *archons* [began to] *mix* their seed with them, *wishing to spoil* them. [But] they *were unable to do so* [for their lack of knowledge concerning how the spirit animates the body and soul]. Then when [you] *these children of the luminosity emerged as forms of light*, they *did so* in *a variety of* ways. *They* each *began* in *their* land [or part of the earth], *making known their special creation before* the *evident* 'synagogue' *made up* of the [fashioned and] modelled forms of *ruin and eternal punishment. And that 'synagogue'* [counterfeit system of belief] was *revealed as having* mixed *within* it, the *root and* seed of the *archons*.

So, we are here to destroy the toils of the archons. By surviving in glory upon the earth, you are a condemnation of him and all their works!

THE HIGH DIVINE 4TH FORM ON EARTH
Human prophets, saints, and martyrs, et al.

(65) Then the *Christos made* [...angels] of them all - and *their* spirits are *clearly* superior because *they are* blessed [meaning graced, gifted, and enlightened] and varying in *type and kind. He* also *made* many other [spiritual, sentient] beings, which have no [archon over them] and are [hence] superior to *all* that *came* before them. *Accordingly*,

there are *four *forms*; three that *are of* the
rulers of the eighth heaven [ogdoad].
However, the fourth *form* is *without a ruler*
and perfect, *indeed* the highest of [them] all.
Because these [are the ones who] *will go
into* the holy *dwelling* of their *creator.* And
they will *rest in peace* [that is] eternal,
[bathed in] *indescribable* glory and
everlasting joy.

*Tartarus, earth, astral and spirit.

What is more, they are [also] *monarchs*
within the mortal *world,* in that they are
everlasting. [By their works on earth] they
will condemn the *archons* of chaos and their
armies.

There are many who incarnate the world over in
every age and epoch that come from the highest realm.
They take on human form to walk amongst us,
demonstrating by example, the works of the Spirit.
Some are famous, but who knows how many are not?
Of the last two millennia, Jesus is, by far, the best
known (See Chapter 4, The Jesus Narrative in other
Traditions,). This point of discussion requires special
attention and investigation on the part of the enquirer.

(66) Now the Word [Christos] that is *over
and above* all beings was sent for *the sake
of this one thing*: that he might *declare the
mystery*. He said, "There is nothing *unseen*

that is not *seen*, and *that which* has not been *known* will be *known*." And these were *directed* to *reveal* what is hidden [meaning the Spirit], and [expose] the seven [great] *archons* of chaos and their *wickedness*. And *so it was that* they were *sentenced* to death.

REVELATIONS AND FORETELLING OF THE END

(67) *Once* all the perfect [spirits had incarnated] *into* the modelled forms [made] by the archons - [they] *revealed* the [one] *indefatigable* truth - they *had no trouble putting* to shame all the *works* of the [shadow] gods. And they *were decreed* to be a *damnation*. And their *powers withered*. Their *supremacy* dissolved. Their *foresight* became *void*, along with their [perceived] *magnificence*.

(68) Before the *completion* of the age, the *earth* will *quake* with great *thunderbolts*. Then the *archons* will be *miserable* [...at] their death. The angels will *grieve* for their *humans*, and the [elemental] demons will *cry* over their *times*, and their *humans* will *moan* and *shout* at their death.

Next within this passage comes the beginning of the new age where their rulers will fall under the influence of the 'fiery sword' of the demiurge, the controller of soul entities. In Eastern Orthodox tradition, after Jesus was crucified and resurrected, the fiery sword was removed from the Garden of Eden, making it possible for humanity to re-enter Paradise. And so, 'intoxicated' by it, *they will declare war on one another so that the earth, too, will become saturated in blood. Then, the celestial sky will stop moving, the seas will turn stormy, the sun will darken, and the moon will no longer shine. The stars will also cease their 'circuits'. Then will come a directed thunderous force and power from above the firmament of the eight heaven where Sophia dwells.*

Claiming responsibility for the product of her embryonic waters, namely, ether and matter, and that which emerged from it, a demiurge, *she will extinguish that 'wise fire' soul of 'intelligence'. She will adorn herself with the garments of wild and boundless rage and chase all the 'gods of chaos' and throw them below 'into the abyss' where they will be annihilated because of all their works.* It likens them to 'volcanoes' consuming one another through and by the hand of the demiurge, until nothing of them is left. He will then turn in on himself and destroy himself out of existence, like the Enochian Watchers.

(69 - 71) Scholarly analysis and retranslation of these, the final three passages of the book, are well executed and can be easily found at Gnosis.org. Copyright restrictions prevent reproduction here, so it has been necessary to precis them below in order to complete the narrative.

> *(69) The collapse of their heavens. Their forces are destroyed by fire. Their lower nightmare realms will be overturned. Yaldabaoth's heaven will be split asunder. His* [realms will] *fall on the* [pillars that] *hold them up. All will go into the abyss. The abyss will be upturned.*

> *(70) Light will fill the darkness like it had*

never existed at all. Matter will be dissolved. The perceived 'deficiency' [or] 'disturbance' will be pulled up by the root and cast into darkness. The cleansing light of destruction will return to its source. The beauty and magnificence of the high angelic forms will appear throughout eternity.

(71) When the scriptures are fulfilled by the prophets, saints, martyrs, masters of light and the 'perfect', those who have fallen short of their measure will be given abode in true heaven, but 'will never enter' the realm of the high angelic ones, for all will go to from where they have come. By what you do, and your own gnosis, you will make your (individual) nature known.

CHAPTER FOUR
FURTHER READING AND AUTHOR COMMENTARY

THE ENTIRE TIMELINE COMPRESSED

For quick reference, here is the timeline of the first part of the Book of Great Secrets.

(1) We live in the 3rd Age of 'chaos'.
(2) The 2nd Age is the 'Age of Chaos' which
    (a) 'originated' from out of something generated by the true God called shadow.
(3) Into chaos, God struck light producing a wonder.

(a) The composition of that wonder which formed from this event was a vast cosmic womb within chaos and was filled with dynamic fluidities.

(b) That womb contained the growing spirit foetuses of the 'aeons' (super gods, generators, and creators).

(c) Once emerged from the womb, the aeons generated spirits and other immortal life forms within their own realms or spheres of influence.

(4) The cosmic womb in which the aeons formed burst open within an area of chaos whose first part is called shadow.

(a) Shadow is the subtle etheric medium, substance or product of the embryonic waters of the womb, which is neither of spirit nor matter but, like the energy of the soul, it exists between the two.

(b) It is also referred to as the 'waters' or developing from the 'waters' which are themselves defined as,

(c) (not wet waters but rather) an invisible complex fluidity that flows within the void.

(d) The 'shadow' 'waters' that burst from His womb reached only so far into the chasm.

(e) And in terms of that fluidity, it is said that everything exists in different states of flow or liquidity.

(5) Concerning the world, two lower aeons emerged from His womb of chaos, Sophia and her male equivalent, Christos. With the forethought and permission of her Father, Sophia decided to act alone when she generated her own womb, meaning without the partnership of her male equivalent, the aeon, Christos. She did this in order to grow her own spirit foetuses of gods and deities, meaning divine energies and intelligences.

(a) Her womb burst open and gave them birth, and they flourished within that area of chaos.

(b) But two other things emerged from her embryonic waters. These were,

> (i) the subtle etheric substances of shadow-ether and dark-ether which formed their own plane of astral-soul-ether and,

> (ii) the substance of matter which formed into the material plane.

(6) The 3rd Age (that of matter within the void of chaos)

> (a) As a product or *'out of'* these substances, matter formed its own plane within an area of chaos beneath etheric shadow and darkness, thereby becoming a part of it but not all of it. And shadow, darkness and matter were projected out, thereby giving rise to all the phenomena of our universe.

HOW THE MAJOR ARCANA TAROT ALIGNS WITH THE GREAT BOOK OF SECRETS

It is possible to piece together enough of the timeline of the Book of Great Secrets from 20 out of 22 of the Major Arcana suit. However, their numerical order must be altered from the orthodox version. Here is a basic outline which also includes their Chaldean numerological significance.

THE EMPRESS.

III: The Empress, Sophia, the great creator goddess. 3 = Ambition. She is sometimes depicted in this card as being pregnant with her hand on her womb representing the cosmos and her embryonic waters.

IV: The Emperor is her husband, Christos of the bridal chamber. 4 = Sensitivity.

IX: The Hermit. 9 = Determination and the material world. Yaldabaoth, her Child of Chaos, who emerged from the bile of her womb, moves across the face of her waters, alone in the void of shadow/darkness until she detects his presence and calls to him.

VIII: Strength. 8 = Misunderstanding. Sophia wrestles to control him, her lion-faced Yaldabaoth. Sometimes he is shown emerging from her abdomen. She will often have an infinity symbol over her head representing eternity.

I: The Magician. 1 = Creation. She makes him the fashioner and maintainer of the etheric and the physical universe by way of wisdom-wizardry. He can make and conjure anything except immortality. This creates colossal envy within him and is represented by the infinity symbol above his head.

XIX: The Sun. 19 = The Sun, God and Man, spirit and material combined, and Prince of Heaven. Sophia, the transforming aeon, creates 1st Adam of the Luminaries, Lucifer the Sun, bringer of light. This is her first stage to cleansing our realm of archons. She transmutes Sabaoth into the sun and, hence, Yaldaboath's 'footstool', the earth, into a realm capable of hosting organic life – the air of which becomes poisonous to them in physical form. He is shown to have a single helix garment, banner or scarf representing the serpent stream of the Zoe ray.

XVIII: The Moon. 18 = Creation, material, and war. Following on from The Sun, as a counter to Sophia's correction, the eclipsing rayed moon drips the blood of war onto the earth where the bloodthirsty dog, wolf, and crab drink of it. And, in terms of Sophia's correction, the lunar disk mathematically squares the circle of the earth, and together with the sun, balances the energies of our world that are essential for the organic life aspect of her Divine Mission Plan.

VII: The Chariot 7 = Independence. This represents the drawing of the planets and constellations across our sky, thereby creating the measure of time. Sometimes the central figure, Kronos the God of Time, holds a sky disk in his left-hand symbolising minutes, hours, days, seasons, and the Earth year.

XVII: The Star. 17 = Peace and Love, the Venusian 8-pointed 'Star of the Magi'. The immortal, superior power. The heavenly bringer of organic life to the earth. '*Rightly*, it has been said: [accomplished] "through the waters." The *Divine female* water vivifies [animates, activates] *everything* [and] purifies it.' Sometimes there is a phoenix visible in the Tree of Life to the right, representing the yet-to-be-created human being.

0: The Fool. Zero = Duration. 'Saklas, the fool', claims a type of credit for all the wonders. He thinks he rules the realm upon which he stands.

XVI: The Tower. 14 = Change and often dangerous elemental upheaval. This could be taken to represent Sophia's casting down of the archons and their leader, Yaldabaoth, into Tartarus after he claimed credit for the new celestial order of things by declaring himself the one and only god. She lets out a thunderbolt thereby creating a celestial and etheric upheaval of the vertically integrated realms of ether and matter. From that moment on, they knew there was a more powerful force than themselves in the universe.

XII: The Hanged Man. 12 = Suffering and mental anxiety. It represents the sacrificing of the human being for the plans of Yaldabaoth. But it also symbolises his fate now that he and his created retinue have been cast below. Archons turn everything upside down. That is why nothing works in the human world for the sake of their influence.

WHEEL of FORTUNE

X: The Wheel of Fortune. 10 = Honour and the inevitability of Divine plans being completed. Further, introduced into the new earth cycle is chance, fate, and fortune and all the things that are beyond human control. The moving wheel is the world, and the people of the earth, ergo, the serpent and the reptile, are attached to it. Its relentless motion cannot be stopped. The yet-to-be-created human being will have no power over it. It is at the behest of the gods to grant or take away good fortune. Starting top left and going clockwise, the four sky corners, or constellations, represent Aquarius in human forms, Scorpio in eagle forms, Leo in lion forms, and Taurus in calf forms.

XV: The Devil. 15 = Manipulation for either good or bad. Yaldabaoth splits the newly created androgyne into male and female. The chain represents the binding together in union with him as the key destructive intercessor. He is sometimes depicted with a burning sun behind him symbolising the shadow he casts over the earthly life. The male and female here represent his version of Sophia's Adam and Eve. The female carries the fruit of the tree, and the male carries the fire of the soul. The demiurge can also be shown with a psychic third eye illustrating the power and access he will have over the human mind and our world.

XIV: Temperance. 14 = The elements. To counter this, Sophia rebalances the energies of the Pistis waters, ergo, the earth and all it contains by way of her Divine Mission Plan. She makes the conditions right for the succeeding Adam and Eve.

THE LOVERS.

VI: The Lovers. 6 = Sensuality and motherliness. With 1st Adam, the sun, Sophia acts as the animating principal in the life of 3rd Adam and Eve. She corrects the error of Yaldabaoth and makes the conditions right for the love that springs eternal from Eros (the midpoint), thereby bringing together the sexual halves in union for the creation of the Anthropos that will be the next stage to her destruction of the archons.

XIII: Death. 13 = "They that understand the number 13 will be given power and dominion." But through Yaldabaoth's intermeddling, the world soon becomes a realm of Death where nothing lasts forever, and all things are characterised by it. It is no respecter of institutions and visits upon both young and old, rich, and poor.

XX: Judgement. 20 = Spiritual and etheric awakening. And when we die, we are summoned by clarion call to it for the weighing of our etheric souls. This applies right across our 3rd Age until its end.

XI: Justice. 11 = Hidden danger, trials, strange fatality, and repetition. Her Libran scales must remain balanced if you are to pass through into the next phase of life. Those who fail are sent back to begin life's path over again, as symbolised by its governing number 11. Judgement also represents her ruling on the archons and all their works. They will never pass into the Spirit Realm. Instead, they will be sent down to the abyss where they will destroy themselves under Yaldabaoth's authority, and then he himself will destroy himself and it will be like they had never existed.

XXI: The World. 21 = Victory after prolonged battles, long initiation, and tests of determination. Sophia will complete her cleansing of this realm and by doing so, claim her Crown of the Universe which none shall take away, symbolised by the number 21. And she will set her seal around the world and 'will bring it into one with the light...*Amen – Sophia – So be it.'*

WHAT THEY DON'T TELL YOU ABOUT GNOSTICS

Gnostics were expert in psychic and spiritual awareness. They were fluent in the ways of the Spirit. They understood the thin divisions in place between Heaven and Earth, mind, body, and spirit as well as the living soul. They were capable of immense critical thought and like Natural Spiritualists, they despised religion, dogma, creed, and ceremony, and took nothing on face value. They also knew that each human being told a unique, special story. And they, like Sophia, rejoiced in life through experimentation, opening-up and cosmic understanding.

There are no Gnostic wars to record because they did not live by the sword. There is no corruption in high places with them because they viewed the growing worldliness of the Church with great suspicion in the same way the as the Coptic. In short, they became extinct by falling victim to that which they warned about from the start!

John Lennon on Gnostics: *"It seems to me that the only true Christians were the Gnostics, who believe in self-knowledge, i.e., becoming Christ themselves, reaching the Christ within, the light is the truth. Turn on the light. All the better to see you with, my dear."*

THE JESUS NARRATIVE IN OTHER TRADITIONS

Jesus? We don't even know who Shakespeare was!

Certain key elements of the story of Jesus occur in other languages, races, cultures, and eras. This can be very confusing for the enquirer when trying to put flesh on the truths that are alive in tales. Jesus's story is not alone in this fact. For instance, the story of the demiurge, as demonstrated in these codices, also has parallels within the Greek tradition. Zeus often imitates the works of Yaldabaoth. And Lucifer also appears in various forms in different myths and legends throughout the world. So, what are we to make of that?

It might be worth considering two things, one of which is the true timeline of historical events. It may surprise you to know that not all scholars, scientists and other professional theorists can agree on dates and identities when it comes to world histories. Like the KJV with its four gospels, they decided that these are the four and only true gospels of the life and times of Jesus. Even in the case of Mary Magdalene, her identity is unknown. It is assumed, without any evidence whatsoever, that she and the woman in the brothel are one and the same. The other thing to consider is that most of what Jesus did, by way of miracles (psychic and spiritual phenomena), were nothing new. They had already been recorded as being accomplished by other prophets in the Old Testament. Concerning the raising of the dead, the prophet Elijah raises a young boy from death in (1 Kings 17:17-24). Elisha raises the son of the Woman of Shunem (2 Kings 4:32-37). And there is the account of the dead man's body that was thrown into Elisha's tomb is resurrected when his body touches the bones of Elisha in (2 Kings 13:21).

Viracocha is described as a bearded Caucasian man who arrived from the east in a boat without oars and had twelves followers with him. He is recorded throughout the Americas as bringing civilisation to the people and performing miracles. And, as with Jesus, there were some places from where he was rejected and chased.

Is it possible that all these stories are the same Jesus in different traditions? And of the twelve chosen ones, these would be different from those who went abroad. And before you dismiss that idea, consider this. There are twenty-one missing years from his life. Are we to believe he went nowhere?

OCEANUS AND PISTIS

In early antiquity, Oceanus was the father of all the gods and the name of the god of the waters, or great river that surrounded the earth. He should not be confused with Poseidon, the Greek god of the sea. However, it is worth noting that in some schools of thought he is demoted to merely a bit part player in the whole Greek pantheon. It all depends on what you believe and to whom you go to for information.

According to M. L. West, the etymology of his name is unclear and cannot be clarified from Greek. The lower status version has him merely as the eldest of the Titan offspring of Uranus (Sky) and Gaia (Earth). So here we have the triad of land, sea, and air. Some have pointed to the Deception of Zeus in the Iliad as signifying Homer's awareness of an earlier tradition where Oceanus and Tethys, and not Uranus and Gaia, were the father and mother of all the gods respectively. Hypnos, the god of sleep, proclaims Oceanus as the 'genesis for all', meaning father of the Titans.

Perhaps Oceanus and his wife, Tethys have found a friend in the NHC Book of Great Secrets and Testament of Norea. According to the NHC, outer space is not empty, but filled with the waters (Pistis) from which everything sprung by that very power. Even today in our technocratic world, there are many who cast doubt on the scientific claim that space is an empty vacuum and is, instead, filled with a type of fluid.

Upon proper construction, it is ludicrous to think that *nothing*, as a *thing*, can have any real existence in our plane of matter. There must always be *something*. Hence, Oceanus and his female equivalent, Tethys, fill the void of chaos.

A COSMIC CATASTROPHE TAKES PLACE

As we immerse ourselves deeper into the cosmology of this book and the subsequent formation of our solar system, one cannot help but draw parallels between this and the work of the Chilean astronomical genius, Farada. He rediscovered our solar system's negative twin sun, *Nemesis,* a dark sun or brown dwarf, 32 billion km beneath the ecliptic plane of our solar system. Ominously, it is also home to the 'destroyer comet-planet *Hercolubus'* which is slingshot out from this region towards our sun approximately every 13,500 years. Like Hercolubus, its brother planetary spheres (or heavens) also have *no light.*

Suffice it to say, at this stage in the timeline, our solar system or Hebdomad of seven Great Archons, shares remarkable similarities to the Nemesis system, both being one and the same system.

(1) *Nemesis & Hercolubus*

(a) Carlos Muñoz Ferrada (1909 - September 11th, 2001) was a truly gifted Chilean scientific genius. For fifty-nine years he startled the world with his super predictive abilities across the disciplines of seismology and astronomy. He first came to prominence on the 19th of January 1939, headlining the newspaper "El Sur" by predicting that just five days later, on the 24th of January at 7.10 pm, his country would experience a massive earthquake. *Sans surprise,* no one believed him. And at 7.10 pm on the day nothing happened. But they did not have long to wait for the predicted disaster to strike. A little over four hours later, at 11.29 pm, it took just 18 seconds to kill 40,000 people! Other well catalogued predictions followed. For example,

1960 A series of earthquakes between 21st and 25th May
1964 The great tsunami that reached Alaska
1965 The big earthquake of Ligua
1985 The big earthquake of Valaparaiso
1986 Halley's Comet would suddenly alter speed and go closer to the Sun.

His special *gnosis* went beyond the comprehension and understanding of many of his scientific contemporaries. Like Velikovsky, he studied and utilised open resources, including the historic record, working longer and harder than most to achieve results of astonishing accuracy. His forecasts applied to climates and geophysics the world over. Not only did he discover many comets and planets, but he was able to forecast and calculate their properties. This included trajectory, mass and other behaviours and characteristics long before they were seen by the world's largest telescopes. And because of his amazing predictive abilities, a change was made in how astronomical discoveries were recognised by the Royal Astronomical Society, England. They cited him for changing its policy from that of crediting the one who first sees the object 'by chance' to the one who first predicts 'by calculation'.

(b) Ferrada made an extensive study, including mapping out with estimations, the orbit of a hitherto little-known bringer of destruction to our solar system (of which it is a part) called Hercolubus, so named by him. *"I called it a comet-planet because it has an* [extreme] *elliptical orbit like a comet and because its mass is as great as a planet. It is a planet with* *a tail."* Despite it being classed as a dead planet orbiting a dead star (or type of brown dwarf), by the standards of our solar system it is a very large sphere, supercharged with cosmic energy and whose behaviours are almost impossible to predict. *"It does not respect the laws of celestial mechanics and travels between our sun and a black sun that is 32 billion km away* [*7.2 times the distance between Pluto and the Sun].*"*

*The canon of 72 significance is discussed a little further on in the text.

It will emerge, as it has done innumerable times before, from a mini constellation; our twin solar system of darkness. Almost invisible to the naked eye, we shall not see it until it is right upon us for the reason that it appears in the dark infrared light spectrum.

It rotates at 92 km per second, but it has three speeds. The second speed is that of 76 km per second, achieved by the body coming closer and therefore under the influence of our sun. *"The full speed it keeps for half of its orbit at 300 km per second. That is 1/1,000th the speed of light. It is very fast!"* Ferrada estimated the nearest Earth pass would be 14 million km. It is approximately 6 times the size of Jupiter, meaning nearly 8,000 times the size of the earth. He stressed that, as before in our history, it is survivable provided we prepare our societies for it.

Mass media and disinformation sources have massively distorted and discredited this story.

(2) *The Electric Universe Theory.*

The Thunderbolts Project and Thunderbolts of the Gods is the brainchild of David Talbott and Wallace Thornhill. They describe it as *'an interdisciplinary collaboration of accredited scientists, independent researchers and interested individuals, established in 2004. Its prime mission is to explore the Electric Universe paradigm... from quantum worlds and biological systems to planetary, stellar, and galactic domains...The Thunderbolts of the Gods Project is a fascinating modern reworking of ancient cosmic catastrophe theory and scientific breakthrough. It posits that from the smallest particle to the largest galactic formation, a web of electrical circuitry connects and unifies all of nature, organizing galaxies, energizing stars, giving birth to planets and, on our own world, controlling weather and animating biological organisms.'*

Talbott and Thornhill produced a seminal open-source film, *Symbols of an Alien Sky* (2012), and a shorter segment from it called, *Episode 2: The Lightning Scarred Planet Mars* (2012), which were extensively broadcast by the UK's Paradigm Shift TV channel. The former illustrates how planetary spheres fire out huge cosmic energies that can destroy or transform planets almost immediately. This was the fate of Mars, but not millions of years ago as conventional science insists, but in recent human memory – a view concordant with Immanual Velikovsky. The latter film identifies the depictions of plasma bolts in the cave paintings of prehistory on every continent.

STAR TREK, GENE RODDENBERRY AND "THE RETURN OF THE ARCHONS"

'Interesting' parallels between this season one episode and the archons of the Nag Hammadi Library texts rediscovered in 1945 which predate the Bible texts by over two centuries.

Star Trek's "The Return of the Archons" episode aired 9th February 1967 in season one of the hit US TV show and was based upon a story by the series creator, Gene Roddenberry (1921-91). Of the original three series, he only wrote six stories and none of the teleplays or scripts, meaning he is the single source and inspiration for this teleplay.

The archons, as delineated in much of the rediscovered late antiquity Nag Hammadi Library (NHL) are, amongst other things, a parasitic super intelligent ancient ET predator species, whose definition in this context had yet to enter the lexicon to any extent. Although the codices were dug up in 1945, it is believed they did not begin to be translated until at least 1947, just nineteen years earlier and were not translated into English until 1977 with a preliminary conversion of the whole discovery. So how did Gene Roddenberry achieve this level of accuracy for this episode?

Despite what the title suggests, 'Archon' and not 'Archons' is the name of a Star Fleet vessel whose ship and crew were lost a century earlier on a planet called Beta III. Beta can mean test, trial or experimental, and are concordant with the themes of the NHL throughout insomuch as the human being is tested, put through trials, and constantly experimented on. 'III' could refer to the '3rd Creation/Age' in which we currently have our existence. The episode is archon-like throughout and the naming of the vessel and not the story's 'artificial intelligence' as Archon(s) should not detract from this.

The USS Enterprise, in attempting to investigate the mysterious disappearance of the USS Archon, finds itself locked in a decaying orbit around the planet. This is symptomatic of the state of mind of the inhabitants below, a race of humans lacking in creativity and intention (running counter to their true human nature) who are controlled by an artificial, super intelligence, millennia old. Roddenberry chose a Victorian model for this society, connoting order, and civility but under the control of sinister hooded "lawgivers" who in turn are controlled by an almost omniscient dictator called Landru, a long dead scientist and philosopher who appears to be based on the NHL Chief Archon or false 'God Almighty' - fashioner and maintainer of the human perceived world.

Each day, when a bell rings, the humans erupt into chaotic practices of savagery, debauchery, and all manner of unspeakable ills, completely belying their alternative passive disposition. One is set against the other in a frenzy of violence and sexual deviancy - even against members of the same family. In other words, they exhibit types of behaviour on which the archons feed. The chime rings out and just as quickly they return to a type of blind normality, albeit that of a continuous collective amnesia. Captain Kirk and his crew try to awaken them from their sleep but to no avail. These indigenous humans have little concept or *gnosis* of what has just taken place and do not see themselves as asleep or under any external influence. This is another theme of the NHL – the sleep and amnesia of the human being.

But they are the preserve of "The Body" of Landru, or the telepathic communal being who has access to their minds - something of which the NHL archons are also masters. The crew of the USS Enterprise eventually manage to break the computer's flawed programming. This homage to the texts is an important plot point for the reason that they stress this as something humanity needs to do. Landru, the original creator of this imperfect plan (or NHL 'experiment') was himself long ago in antiquity, an organic human, i.e., made in the image of a higher God. But this defective program, like the Divine Eco Feminine Sophia's creation of the Chief Archon in the texts, was a mistake made on the part of genuine motive. This 'error' developed into an inorganic Landru copy, becoming a pitiless and bleak archon predator and the humans nothing more than sterile slaves controlled by his instigated underlings. This episode also contained the first reference to the motif, theme, and philosophy of the Prime Directive, which would go on to characterise the franchise throughout its many incarnations.

Gene Roddenberry is a somewhat enigmatic character despite his perceived public persona. The Return of the Archons episode gives a good and clear indication that the true contents of the Nag Hammadi texts were well understood in certain elite circles (many of which he comfortably navigated) before they were translated.

'The Star Trek Conspiracy - Part One' (June 2012), hosted on the UK-based Truth Seeker's Guide website authored by Carl (the 'Guide') is a consummate piece, detailing and outlining some of Gene Roddenberry's lesser well-known connections and interests not found in the official sanitised biographies, fan sites or Wikipedia. These include the secret work of Lab9 and his extensive sinister associations with NASA.

WORLD LEADERS AND THE ARCHONS OF CONTROL

This subject will be dealt with in more detail in future books in this series. But for now, it is enough to say that 'evil' world leaders are fully aware of archon control over the human being; indeed, they facilitate their intrusions wherever they can like obedient co-workers. They have contracted with the archons from the start. To the flawed human being, the archons offer power and secret knowledge. The controlling powers of Earth's elites have struck deals with them at the expense of all others. Like with the temptation of Christ, they offer their faithful immense rewards that exploit the negative trait of greed they sewed into the tree of the human soul in the beginning.

In that part of the afterlife over which they exercise most control, namely the lower nightmare etheric plane, they imprison human souls, ergo spirits, that have imitated or knowingly carried out their works whilst incarnated in the physical body. The afterlife they promise to the demonic world elites turns out to be one of endless fear, torture, and threat of destruction. The eternal progress that is normally open to every human soul is cut short here because under the natural laws of spirit, they have found themselves in a world they have made for themselves.

The masters of deception promise them the earth and all the things thereof because it is, for the most part, theirs to give, save for we, the Divine incarnated, immortal spirits who knowingly walk upon it as a condemnation of them in the light of Sophia and Christos.

HOW TO PROTECT YOURSELF AGAINST ARCHON INTRUSION AND ABDUCTION

If you have read and understood this book properly then it is not hard to do. Firstly, you *are* the control. You have nothing to fear. They want you to be frightened. They have no power over you unless you give it to them.

In the physical form, say, in your home, you may suddenly become aware of their strange energy and, indeed, presence. It may feel unhuman, i.e., that you are not dealing with the discarnate spirit of someone passed away, or a haunting event. What you experience instead is a deep, dark intelligence that is testing you. It will have a strange and disturbing curiosity for you, in what makes you, and what you are. It is what this author calls archon interrogation of the soul, and it goes deep. They want to see if you are waking up like Adam and Eve in the original garden. They fear an awakening in you; that you should ever become alive to their presence and their intentions.

Do not worry. You are not alone in this experience. And you will be glad to know there is an instant cure. You should say out loud, or in your mind, that you are aware of their intrusion and that you know why they are there. You should then inform them that you come from the pre-existing God, and your home is in the Spirit, with the Spirit. Tell them they have no place with you and that you command them by the Power of the Spirit, or the Power of Sophia/Christos, to go back to the realm from which they came, and that they are not to return to you. This commandment by you will fill them with fear. You cannot reason with archons and demonic entities because they have no reason within them.

For example, there is a tale which goes something like this. Yaldabaoth created the beasts and the human. One of his sons said there is an imbalance because the beasts lack rationality whereas the humans have it in abundance. So, to redress this he turned some of the beasts into humans. That is why some may have human form but the souls of beasts. They are like the crocodile who ate the frog he helped across the river after promising not to do so. When asked why, he replied that it was in his predator nature! They are incapable of change and fear it in the human being.

Next, if you should find yourself intruded upon in the astral dream state, then the cure is essentially the same as previously discussed. However, the astral offers a different set of problems to that of the physical realm, namely that they are more in control over there in terms of inflicting mental torture, anxiety, and navigational control of your experience. You may feel more trapped and incapable of escape in this condition. But do not worry. This is exactly how they want you. Prior to going to sleep you should command them not to visit upon you either by waking you up or in the sleep state. You need only empower the Divine Creation Spirit to protect you throughout your night.

Sometimes you may encounter archons as UFOs. They may even follow you. They will be aware that you can see them. Sometimes this can be a strategy of theirs to prime you for a nocturnal visitation. If you are alone during an encounter, then stand your ground and inform them through your mind that they cannot seize you because of your home in the Spirit where dwells the immortal pre-existing One. Not only are you the control, but you have sovereignty and dominion over this realm whereas they do not for the sake of not belonging in the material biological realm of the earth plane.

(Fig. 20) A fragment of the Gospel of Judas Iscariot.

A-Z GLOSSARY OF TERMS

Anthropos. A human being of God.

Authorities. Archons and the Seven Great Archons.

Aeon. Super gods, generators, or creators such as Christos or Sophia. They inhabit the heavenly planes of the 9th ennead and oversee all below it. They are androgynous though can favour male or female, positive or negative polarities. They can act alone or in union with one another. They exist outside of space and time as well as within it. They are the true creators of the human being and are credited with creating our spirits too, albeit by way of the Entire Creator.

Almighty God. (See Demiurge). Chief Archon, the Abrahamic 'God' of the Old Testament, false, fake, counterfeit (Yahweh, Jehovah, etc). From *El-Mighty* or *Mighty El* - a shortened form of Mighty Elemental God, God of the Elements, meaning matter and ether.

Apocalypse. Old English, via Old French and ecclesiastical Latin from Greek *apokalupsis*, from *apokaluptein* 'uncover, reveal', from *apo-* 'un-' + *kaluptein* 'to cover'.

Archons. The pre-existing species to the human being that emerged from the bile of Sophia's womb. They inhabit the planes of matter and ether. They have a colossal envy of the human being. They can take on physical form and move through ether and matter unimpeded like fish through water. They exist in several forms. They can be reptilian (three colour types), prenatal, meaning 'like an unborn foetus.' This can be extended to insectoid ('ant people') and alien greys. They can also take on human form. In whatever form they take, they lack a spirit within them. This is the single cause of all their envy towards the human being and the reason for their constant experimentation and intrusion. They are desperate to understand how the spirit of the human being incarnates and animates the etheric soul and the physical body. They are rulers of the earth and the lower nightmare level where the souls of human beings are sent if they have imitated their works.

Belief. *Beliefs* are what destroy the world. The Gnostics say you either know or you do not know. They viewed with derision, people, institutions, and religions whose aim was to persuade you, often against your will, to believe what they believe.

Breath or **Breathe**. Soul and life. *Principal animating breath* to the physical body.

Christos. Male aeon. The model for 'perfect human', Jesus Christ.

Cloud. Sometimes taken to mean the galactic cloud and ogdoad, the former being visible to the naked eye as the Milky Way. But in some codices, such as Judas, it can also mean the generating womb from which all manner of aeons, gods and deities emerged. It all depends on the context and setting in which the term is used.

Darkness. Let there be *dark* and lo there was! The void of chaos, the chasm, and (sometimes) the inky black void.

Death. Where this word occurs as a proper noun, it is taken to mean that the realm of matter is mortal where nothing can last forever. It is the defining characteristic of the physical realm. Like the realms that are above, everything would live forever were it not for the sake of it. It is a creation and biproduct of the archons' mischief.

Demiurge. (Artisan). Also see *Almighty God, Yaldabaoth, Saklas, Samael, Chief Archon, Ruler.* Although androgynous, the demiurge is considered a male energy. He is the illegitimate (hence deficient) son of Sophia who emerged out of the cosmic fluid (or 'bile') of her womb. He is made of a substance, higher than matter, called shadow, meaning ether, and hence *'with no spirit in him'*. She makes him a princely ruler, fashioner, and maintainer of both the shadow and physical world. His power and influence extend to the lower etheric nightmare plane where human souls are destined to go should they do the work of the archons, whether having gnosis of the same or not. He and his created retinue *can* act as a barrier to souls accessing the higher astral realm that leads to the Spirit World upon death of the physical body, but only if those returning spirits have been soiled by archon influence.

Desire. (*Himireris* and sometimes *Eros*). It exists between the hemispheric states of love and hate of the human being. It can also dwell almost exclusively in either sphere of their soul, amplifying either feature.

Divine Mission Plan. We are incarnated to the earth to destroy the work of the false, self-proclaimed creator and all his retinue. This is a spiritual war to cleanse this realm of matter and ether and 'bring it into one with the light.' The texts make it clear that by simply being here, 'you are a condemnation of them and all their works!'

Envy. The absolute destruction of that which the archons cannot have, possess, or control for themselves.

Eros. Not a sentient being, rather an emotional trait of the soul etheric, linked to the desire that springs eternal between the sexual halves, bringing them together in union.

Eve. Life. Aka Zoe and Pronoia. A name given to the female personification of Sophia's life force. She is an energy of super complexity that exists in several forms as a female counterpart, 'bride' or 'wife' to (1st Adam of light) he of the name Sabaoth (Lucifer) and called 'Zoe'. With (2nd Adam of soul) Satan as Pronoia and with the androgyne (3rd Adam of the earth) as Eve of the Anthropos body.

Fruit. The illumined and illuminating product of the sacred trees, which themselves are the realisation of the Godhead's formulation and plan.

Generation. (Partly weasel). A term often chosen instead of *creation,* to divorce you further from God and His Truth. Sometimes used to distort a meaning. Consider one or the other when encountering it in the 'authorised' texts. *Generation* implies a twenty-five-year span of human experience, whereas *creation* gives a wider implication as to the meanings one can derive from the library overall.

Gods and Deities. They are principally the product of Sophia's womb and secondarily the product of the womb of Yaldabaoth (the Abrahamic God). These are not to be taken as living beings similar to humans, and neither should they be defined in human terms. Moreover, they can be thought of as the constituent parts of creation such as laws, energies, properties, characteristics, qualities, features of the soul, the material and astral worlds. They can also be observable heavenly bodies such as Lucifer the sun, as well as (for example) Desire (Eros), which can be understood to be the *'primal pleasure* [that] *blossomed* between all the gender opposites of the living things of the earth.'

Heavens. Realms, worlds and spheres or planets, namely of the hebdomad, especially when taken to mean solar system.

7th Heaven is the *hebdomad* or seven Great Archons and visible solar system

8th Heaven is the *ogdoad*, astral realm, and galaxy/Milky Way.

9th Heaven is the *ennead* or realm of Sophia and the Christos. It is from here we are said to have originated and to where we shall return upon the death of our physical body, provided we have not imitated the work of the archons by causing loss, harm or damage and created no victims.

Hebdomad. The solar system, seven heavenly bodies, or realm of the seven Great Archons. The ancients observed that against the sphere of the fixed stars, i.e., the ogdoad or galaxy, seven other bodies moved independent of it. Two were the discs of the moon and sun, and five were the 'wandering stars' of Mercury, Venus, Mars, Jupiter, and Saturn. All are visible to the naked eye.

Holy Spirit. The Divine Female Principal Power of Sophia. For instance, in the Gospel of Philip, paragraph 17, *Some said that Mary conceived by the Holy Spirit. They are in error. They do not understand what they say. When did a woman ever conceive by a woman?* Hence, the Holy Spirit is Sophia.

Hypostasis (of the Archons/Reality of the Rulers). This book has been misnamed. Its true title is found in the *Book of Great Secrets,* paragraph 10 and 11, as *Account of Noraia* and *Account of Oraia* respectively. The term *hypostasis* does not appear in the original translation.

(Wiki). (Greek: ὑπόστασις, *hypóstasis*) is the underlying state or underlying substance and is the fundamental reality that supports all else. In Neoplatonism the hypostasis of the soul, the intellect (*nous*) and "the one" was addressed by Plotinus.

Incorruptibility. That which is *not* made of matter such as ether, the soul, and the spirit and therefore not subject to decay.

Liberator. (Also see Saviour). Considered by this author to be a more accurate translation than *saviour,* especially seeing as the texts pre-date the use of this term! In the orthodox bible, Jesus describes himself as the Son of Man, not God. In the NHC he comes as the liberator and 'perfect human being' to reveal God to you and you to yourself. Namely, that you will do all the works that he does and greater – 'greater works' will follow those who follow his example.

Mansions. 'In my Father's house there are many mansions,' said Jesus. These are the astrological houses of the 7th and 8th heavens, subdivided into twelve houses/mansions.

Matter. In the Mary codex Jesus answers, *"Each life, each moulded form, each living thing, exists in relation* *to everything else."* Matter is heavy and of a lower vibration. So, what *is* matter? When examined under laboratory conditions, fundamental and subatomic particles are, in fact, found to be hollow. So whatever matter is, it is not solid! Jesus, in the Mary codex, says about matter that *it dissolves into that which is of itself.*

Monad. 1st. First.

Natural Spiritualism. Not to be confused with 'spiritualism' or the Spiritualism practiced as a religion in churches or what is demonstrated by psychics on stage and TV. In short, it is the natural ability of people to discern for themselves the laws and principles of that which exists beyond the five senses of the physical world, free from any intercessor, church, temple or religiosity. Natural Spiritualism is a term created by this author in his book, (West, Kevin) *The Psychic and Spiritual Awareness Manual, 6th Books,* (2014).

Oceanus. The importance of Oceanus cannot be underestimated. He is the Greek god of the waters that surround the earth. Not to be confused with Poseidon (Greek) or Neptune (Roman) who were predominantly gods of the seas. (See Chapter Four, *Oceanus and Pistis*).

Ogdoad. Meaning eight, 8th heaven, oftentimes cloud or the galaxy/Milky Way. The ancients saw the stars of the galaxy as appearing fixed to the naked eye like the inside of a dome.

Paradise. Not always a geographical location or material place, rather a state of being, to wit, the lit-up Tree of Life and Tree of Knowledge *within* the human. It is also a place where the archons attack the human spirit. To fall or be removed from Paradise is the act of making oneself incompatible with that state of being, either by one's own volition or by the temptation of another. The lit-up tree represents the uninterrupted connection with the Godhead, i.e., the 'perfect human' spoken about by Jesus in the Judas and Mary codices. It is also referred to in the *Book of Great Secrets* as a physical place situated on the peak of Mount Sir (modern day Mount Hermon), at 33° north.

Poverty. The material and spiritually 'deficient' realm of matter, extended to include the substances of shadow and darkness.

Pistis. The personification and manifestation of God's power and will. Also, fluidity.

Pleroma. (1) The spiritual universe as the dwelling place of God and as the complete realisation and expression of Divine powers and emanations. (2) The entirety of the Godhead that resides in (the) Christos, totality, unity, fullness. The Divine centre of pureness and incorruptibility.

Pronoia. Negative Zoe. Daughter of Yaldabaoth. She is responsible for creating *his* version of *life.*

Reflection. This means similar to, and can sometimes mean replication.

Replication. The pattern of life and creation.

Root. (Chakra), of the trees of *life* and *knowledge,* and also the heavenly realm from whence we have come.

Rulers. (plural) also archons. Singular, 'The ruler', see Demiurge.

Sabaoth. One of the seven Great Archons, a child of the demiurge who was transformed by Sophia from a sphere of darkness into the sun of the solar system (Lucifer, 1st Adam). Also meaning Sabbath - 'day of rest', Age of the Sun - Sunday.

Saklas. Foolish god, the demiurge.

Samael. Blind god, god of the blind, the demiurge.

Saviour. (See Liberator).

Shadow. A super complex, intelligent medium made of the subtlest ether. It is not spirit or matter but exists between the two. It is also the substance from which the human soul and the demiurge are made. It is the substance or product of the embryonic waters of the cosmic womb.

Sin. Error, wrongdoing. In the Judas codex, Judas asks Jesus what is the sin of the world? Jesus replies that there is no sin without you to create it. So, perhaps *all* the sin in the world is created by the human being and the archons merely feed from it.

Sophia. (Also see Wisdom). Her name means love and faith. Androgynous aeon favouring the female half of the helix. She can act alone as well as in partnership with her masculine equal, Christos. She emerged from the power of the Entire Creator and the hierarchy of the 72 planes to reside in the ennead or 9th heavenly plane. She is our mother. Where the Virgin Mary, Mother of God, is concerned, this would appear as a huge distortion. Sophia is the virgin mother.

Soul. (*Shadow*) Made of the subtlest ether, meaning it is neither spirit nor matter but somehow exists between the two. It is made by the archons from a template (mischievously) given to them by Sophia. It is created from a substance that emerged from the embryonic waters of her womb. It *can* be immortal and alterable. It is formed from the substance of *shadow* by the archons as a vehicle for the human spirit and animator of the physical body. It is a super complex energy form comprising a system of seven sacred organs, or chakras, as well as meridians, intelligence, and auras.

Spirit and spirit. God and human.

Sunday. *Sun-god.* Day means deity or God/god, and can also mean Age or Age of, depending on the context in which it is used. So, Mon-day is moon-god like Satur-day is Saturn-god.

Tartarus. Sometimes spelled Tartaros in the NHC. It is a jail or pit where the souls of the wicked reside in perpetuity and is overseen by the archons and their leader. (Chapter Two, paragraph 13).

Tripartite. Can be taken to mean a division between the Pure, the Ornate and the Grotesque. Almost exclusively in the NHC, it can be used to describe the three constituent parts of the 'human being', namely, the spirit, the soul, and the physical body.

Verbal Expression. (Weasel). A type of formulation and plan according to natural laws. *Verbal* being the word, the truth, the law, and *expression* being the outcome of it.

Vibration. A level of consciousness, and sometimes resonance.

Virgin. (Helix) Single and without entwinement or union with another.

Wisdom. A term that meant something else back in the time of Jesus. Often taken to mean gnosis, power and law. But it may more accurately be thought of as the ability to create. To wit, a type of *wizardry.* The texts describe the Beast in the garden as the 'wisest of all the beasts' because he was the best made! Therefore, wisdom, throughout the NHC, should be taken to mean that which is created and made. This is why the demiurge can sometimes be said to have wisdom.

Yaldabaoth/Yaltabaoth. See Demiurge.

Zoe. See Eve.

IMAGES AND SOURCES USED

Cover art and design by Kevin O'Doherty

Fig. 1
Map of Egypt adapted by Kevin O'Doherty
Fig. 2
Soul Illustration by Kevin O'Doherty
Fig. 3
The Devil, Pamela Colman Smith
Fig. 4
The System of the Soul adapted by Kevin O'Doherty
Fig. 5
The Apple-Shaped Torus Field by Kevin O'Doherty
Fig. 6
Auras by Kevin O'Doherty
Fig. 7
Archons in Prenatal Form composited by Kevin O'Doherty
Fig. 8
Wiki Flammarion adapted by Kevin O'Doherty
Fig. 9
The Chariot, Pamela Colman Smith, adapted by Kevin O'Doherty
Fig. 10
The Prague Astronomical Clock graphic by Kevin O'Doherty based on
eo:Vikipediisto:Maksim (2006)
Fig. 11
The World, Pamela Colman Smith, adapted by Kevin O'Doherty
Fig. 12
The moon squares the circle of the earth graphic by Kevin O'Doherty
Fig. 13
The Lovers, Pamela Colman Smith, adapted by Kevin O'Doherty
Fig. 14
Judgement, Pamela Colman Smith
Fig. 15
Justice, Pamela Colman Smith, adapted by Kevin D O'Doherty
Fig. 16
Justice Maat, photo credit Kevin O'Doherty
Fig. 17

Sumerian Tree of Life, photo credit Kevin O'Doherty
Fig. 18
The Tower, Pamela Colman Smith
Fig. 19
The Phoenix, photo credit Kevin O'Doherty
Fig. 20
A fragment of the Gospel of Judas Iscariot, Tchacos, Wiki Commons.

Printed sources:

West, Kevin, (2014), *The Psychic & Spiritual Awareness Manual*, 6th Books.

Major Arcana tarot illustrations are from *The Original Rider Waite Tarot Deck* first published in 1909. They were conceived by A. E. Waite and designed by English artist Pamela Colman Smith (1878-1951).

Valles, Dr. Jaques, (19th March 2014), *Confrontations*, p.13, Anomalist Books.

Rev. Elliott, G Maurice, (1938), *When Prophets Spoke, Spiritualism in the Old Testament*, Psychic Press, UK.

Mead, G. R. S., (1896), *Pistis Sophia*, Introduction, p. xxxii.

Digital sources:

O'Doherty, Dermot Kevin, (18th May 2022), *Gene Roddenberry and the Return of the Archons*, https://odoherty.substack.com/p/star-trek-gene-roddenberry-and-the?r=rge95&s=w&utm_campaign=post&utm_medium=web

O'Doherty, Dermot Kevin, *Natural Spiritualism, pt 1-3,* (Video playlist), online, 30th May 2020 – 20th January 2021, https://www.youtube.com/playlist?list=PLVCzi1325Tq_4SIYGXmoGPzls1kDwuf52

Gnostic Society, *The Gnosis Archive,* online, updated 2018, accessed 8th June 2022.

Meyer, Marvin W., (2007), *The Nag Hammadi Scriptures*, (ebook), HarperOne; 1st edition, (14th September 2010).

David Flynn, (2005), *The Earth Mars Connection,* online, WFPCo channel, https://youtu.be/ZRXdiqqh82Y

Other books by Kevin Dermot O'Doherty:
The Psychic & Spiritual Awareness Manual (Kevin West)
Mersey Street (novel)
Drac Attack! (children's novella)

Egyptian Nag Hammadi Secrets

All rights reserved © 2022 Kevin Dermot O'Doherty

NOTES

NOTES

.

Printed in Great Britain
by Amazon

29388383R00119